Inspiring Words for Sky and Space Women

Advice from Historic and Contemporary Trailblazers

Cover Photograph Credits

Top Row: (left to right)
Southwest Airlines *Nikki Sereika*, as a member of the Tech Operations and Maintenance team, insures equipment is working efficiently and safely. Many opportunities are available in this critical area of aviation. (Courtesy Southwest Airlines)

Kathryn "Kat" Yancey LaBorie, United Airline Flight 175 Head Flight Attendant, killed on September 11, 2001 when al-Qaeda terrorists flew the Boeing 767-200 with all passengers and crew into The South Tower of the World Trade Center in New York City. In the late 1980s, as an executive at Front Range Airport, Kathryn was the first woman elected President of the Colorado Airport Operators Association. (Gene and Flo Yancey Collection)

Women Airline Pilots; *Kasey Trujillo, Emily Warner, Beverly Sinclair, Donna Miller* before the 2014 National Aviation Hall of Fame ceremony where Warner was inducted. (Hamilton photograph)

Bottom Row: (left to right)
All female International Space Station team from top right clockwise: Japan Exploration Agency astronaut, *Naoko Yamazaki*, NASA astronauts *Stephanie Wilson, Tracy Caldwell Dyson*, and *Dorothy Metcalf-Lindenburger*. (NASA archive)

JaNette Lefkowitz, an accomplished skydiver, won gold at the World Parachuting Championships as a member of our U.S. Women's Team, the Army Golden Knights. (Martha Gough photograph)

Martha Elizabeth McSally with her A-10 Thunderbolt II. In 1988, Martha McSally graduated for the United States Air Force Academy. McSally was America's first woman to fly a fighter jet in combat and the first woman in U.S. history to command a fighter squadron, also in combat. She deployed six times to the Middle East and Afghanistan, flying 325 combat hours in the A-10 "Warthog," earning a Bronze Star and six Air Medals. After a 26-year military career, retiring at the rank of Colonel, she later was elected to the U.S. House of Representatives. She is currently serving in the U.S. Senate representing Arizona. (U.S. Air Force archival photo)

Inspiring Words for Sky and Space Women

Advice from Historic and Contemporary Trailblazers

Penny Rafferty Hamilton, Ph.D.

Mountaintop Legacy Press
Lake Granby, Colorado

The author has made every effort to acknowledge sources and individuals, where appropriate. All capitalization, italics, and other emphasis markings appear as in the cited source or as received by the author. If any information is incorrectly attributed or references/citations are incorrect, please inform the author so the information can be updated correctly in future editions.

Inspiring Words for Sky and Space Women
First Edition
Copyright @ 2020, Penny Rafferty Hamilton, Ph.D.

Published by Mountaintop Legacy Press
ISBN: 978-0-578-78999-6

This book is dedicated to the memory of:

And, to Kathryn "Kat" Yancey LaBorie, United Airlines Flight 175 Head Flight Attendant, killed on September 11, 2001 at 9:03AM ET when al-Qaeda terrorists flew the Boeing 767-200 with all passengers and crew into The South Tower of the World Trade Center.

"May we never forget!"

And, to Emily Howell Warner, who opened America's airline flight decks for women pilots.

TABLE OF CONTENTS

ACKNOWLEDGEMENTS

Thank you to all the inspiring women and publications quoted in this book. I am grateful to my own encouragement team members: Julie Filucci, Lara Kaufmann, Bill Hamilton, Betty Heid, Cindy Irish, Gretchen Jahn, Donna Miller, Gordon Page, Margot Plummer, Tess Riley, Shanon Searls, Kim Stevens, Ann Stricklin, and Jill Tietjen. Special thanks to Patty Wagstaff, Amy Spowart, and Allison McKay, and Joe Clark/ BlueWater Press, LLC.

Thanks to Denver International Airport staff, especially Stacey Stegman, for photographs. Southwest Airlines team members supported research and female team member photographs, especially Michelle Agnew and Renata D'Elena. Special thanks to the many archives for access to historic information and photographs. To our publishing and graphics designer, Patricia Shapiro Book Publishing, I am so grateful for her creative spirit and talent combined with infinite patience for my many and varied projects.

Lastly, thank you to the sponsors, donors, and the selection committee of the 2020 Women in Aviation International Pat Luebke Memorial Scholarship for my Personal Development Award which helped underwrite this research.

1
Welcome to the Sky and Space Sisterhood

There is more to life than being a passenger.
~ Amelia Earhart

Let's just face it. Historically, the air and aerospace industry has not welcomed women with open arms. Fortunately, this is changing. The pioneering women of sky and space have earned their place in the pantheon of aviation greats. Today, they are joined by "their sisters" in this awesome industry. This book tells their stories and shares their advice and words of wisdom. According to the dictionary, "inspire" is a verb meaning to "fill someone with the urge to do something, especially something creative or important." My dream is that everyone reading this book will find inspiration to follow their own dream.

As I researched the stories of the many women for this book, I was immediately struck with the clear message that aviation and aerospace attracts high achievers with "can do" personalities and are possibility thinkers. Although sky and space dreamers, they are very focused and flexible.

Very few women in the industry will tell you being the only woman in the class, conference, or flight deck, is a welcoming or fun experience. By our socialization, women tend to enjoy being team members. Often, we share our feelings and emotions. Usually we actually like talking things out.

One of my best aviation friends was Emily Howell Warner, America's first modern female airline pilot hired by a scheduled Jet-equipped airline. She shared what is was like in those early days breaking the glass ceiling of the airline flight deck. In 1973, Frontier Airlines hired her as their very first female airline pilot. When asked about being the first and only woman to join the Airline Pilots Association (ALPA), the then all-male aviation fraternity, she said she often thought about Eleanor Roosevelt's quote, "Women are like tea bags. We don't know our true strength until we are in hot water!"

Emily had been the flight instructor for many of the men flying for Frontier. Once Frontier hired her, Emily knew if she just continued to do her job well eventually the male airline pilots, flight crews, and passengers would accept her. And, slowly they did. Being the first woman anything puts an enormous burden on that person because she must prove daily she can do the job. Emily told me she was inspired by the brave Women Airforce Service Pilots (WASP), and by her friendships in the International Ninety-Nines.

Even Amelia Earhart needed to be inspired. Research in *Fly Girls, How Five Daring Women Defied All Odds and Made Aviation History*, revealed Amelia kept a scrapbook filled with newspaper clippings about important women making news. Research indicates that how you see yourself impacts your success. Visualizing your success is important for moving toward your goal. It is said, "The me I see is the me I will be." If your goal is to be a pilot, keep a photo of you in or near a plane and display it where it constantly reminds you of your goal. Focus on other successful women in the career you want.

In their book, *Work with Me*, writers Barbara Annis and John Gray found 82% of the women in their research reported they felt some form of exclusion in business, social events, casual meetings, in conversations, or in receiving direct feedback. Feeling isolation in aviation and aerospace careers is not unique.

Your thoughts are powerful. Guard and direct them by constantly feeding positive words and advice to your mind daily. My "Teaching Women to Fly Research Project" found women perform best in an encouraging environment. Two of the top ten ways to increase success for women in aviation were expanding the use of female role models and increasing awareness of historic aviation heroines and their accomplishments. After reading their inspiring stories in this book, no young woman should ever doubt her worth to the air and aerospace industry.

These "her stories" demonstrate the success of these outstanding women in our air and space history. Believe in your own dreams. Daily, create your own world of "good thoughts" by reading the words and stories of our air and space sisters. They have blazed the trail in their own ways to the stars. Authentic stories connect us to others who teach us how to navigate. You will be inspired by the obstacles so many of them overcame. Their words and accomplishments are shared in the chapters with each woman listed alphabetically by last name. Use this book daily to feed your mind with new and inspirational thoughts.

A long "Explore More" chapter of books and organizations encourages you to look into the lives of many who made a path for us all to follow. Books for very young readers are also included. These "her stories" are often hidden in the written history of air and space. Think of the words from these historic and space-age women as important daily advice from your mentors in your "Sisterhood of Sky and Space."

Remember, when one woman achieves, all women achieve. Keep reaching for the stars no matter the journey and destination you choose.

(Pilots of Southwest Airlines. Courtesy of Southwest Airlines)

2
A-Alpha to B-Bravo

*To most people, the sky is the limit. To those who love
aviation, the sky is home. ~ Jerry Crawford*

Abdennebi, Narjess
"My awe and passion for aviation began as a child, ignited by my
favorite book, *The Little Prince*. In the years since, I've woven a career
that has united the technical aspects of aviation, through my work as an
aeronautical engineer, with its management aspects, having bolstered
my Master's degree in air transport management with a PhD in air
transport economics. Moreover, throughout my career in the world of
aviation and travel, I have tried to diversify my knowledge by being
acquainted with the greatest possible variety of stakeholders, such as
airline, travel agency, aircraft manufacturer in the areas of forecasting,
marketing, sales, aftersales support, and licensed personnel training.
This journey and this enthusiasm for all things aviation has brought me
to ICAO." ICAO (International Civil Aviation Organization) is a
specialized Agency of the United Nations. Quote from
www.icao.int/about-icao/women-in-aviation. (The book, *The Little
Prince*, by French aviator, Antoine de Saint-Exupery, is one of the best-
selling and most translated books in the world.)

Andre, Babette
"Of the various endeavors I've undertaken in my checkered careers,
nothing has provided more continual challenge, growth, and personal

fulfillment than aviation. Its horizons are limitless, and it provides better than average career opportunities for women, plus a most auspicious male-female ratio!" Written by Babette in the June 1981, *the 99news* national magazine, "I'd rather be FLYING!" In 1959, Andre graduated from high school in Hawaii before heading to the University of California for her BA with studies in photojournalism, political science, international relations, and French. Next was the Central African country of Cameroun as a two-year Peace Corps volunteer. In 1968, she landed in Colorado where she blazed a wide trail in aviation. She became a pilot to overcome her fear of flying. It must have worked because all these years she has promoted flying. With advanced education and ratings, she became a General Aviation flight instructor, charter pilot, and FAA Accident Prevention Counselor specializing in mountain flying. She became a Gold Seal Flight Instructor, along with founding *Wings West* magazine. She received the National Air Transportation Association Aviation Journalism Award. In 1987, Babette created Colorado's first State Aeronautical Chart. As a Denver KOA radio Sky Watch air traffic reporter, she multi-tasked using her strong aviation and communication skills to fly the airplane, watch out for aviation traffic, spot road traffic delays, speak in 30 second reports, and constantly listen to KOA in case the studio suddenly "cut to you Sky Spy!" For over 43 years, Babette Andre has enjoyed General Aviation flight instructing. For twenty years, she was on the Metro State University Aviation and Aerospace faculty. In 1990, Babette Andre was inducted into the Colorado Aviation Hall of Fame. In 2014, she joined the AOPA national community team as Rocky Mountain Metropolitan Airport's Support Network Volunteer.

The day you give up on your dreams is the day you give up on yourself. ~ Unknown

(Babette Andre Sky Spy. Photograph courtesy Babette Andre)

Armour, Vernice "FlyGirl"

"You wouldn't believe how many times someone has told me they lost their dream, are too busy taking care of everyone else and don't know HOW to take care of themselves anymore, or even worse, they felt guilty taking care of themselves!" ~ www.VerniceArmour.com.

In 2001, Vernice earned her wings as the first African American female pilot for the U.S. Marine Corps. She flew the AH-1W SuperCobra in Operation Iraqi Freedom. Vernice is now an author and public speaker.

Arnold, Sarah

"Running a gliderport takes copious amounts of time and energy, and I sometimes find my passion flagging, the joy forgotten. I crave the glorious solitude of the sky; those secret sunlit spaces which still my soul. So I keep a piece of aviation just for me. Competition soaring restores the romance of flight and reinvigorates my desire to share the joy of aviating with everyone." Quoted in March 2015, EAA *Sport Aviation Magazine*, "Women in the Field: Grassroots Aviators Inspiring Others," by Sparky Barnes Sargent. Aviation became Sarah's passion in childhood. First ultralights, then airplanes. She earned her private at age 17. She enrolled in A&P school. She gained an instrument rating and commercial certificate. In 2003, Sarah discovered soaring. At 24, she bought the Chilhowee Gliderport in Benton, Tennessee. In 2005, Sarah set the U.S. and New Mexico records for distance. In 2008, altitude record was next. In 2011, she set 11 Tennessee and three U.S. records, and became the Sport Class and Club Class National Champion. The world was next. In 2013, Sarah Arnold earned a bronze at the FAI Women's World Gliding Championship. Soaring Society of America provides information on the training in this fascinating sky sport.

Aunon-Chancellor, Serena

"Always follow your passion. If you go down a path you think others want you to follow, you'll be miserable. What you love is your passion, and everything else will work out." Quoted in September 19, 2013 on http://nbclatino.com "Innovator: Serena Aunon, Physician and Astronaut' by Kristina Puga. In 2006, Serena joined the NASA team as a Flight Surgeon spending nine months in Russia's Star City, supporting medical operations for International Space Station crew members. In 2009, she was selected as a NASA-astronaut in our 20th astronaut class of 14 members. In 2010-11, Dr. Aunon-Chancellor was selected for the two-month Antarctica ANSMET expedition to explore that continent and collect meteorites. In 2012, she piloted a NASA/NOAA NEEMO submersible for underwater exploration in Florida. By 2015, she became an aquanaut crew member. In 2018, Astronaut Aunon-Chancellor went back to outer space on the International Space Station clocking 196 days. She is one well-travelled woman explorer.

(NASA Serena Aunon-Chancellor in space. Courtesy of NASA.)

Azara, Laura

"I love the different clients, the fact that they're not just an anonymous face in a crowd in the back of the airplane, and that I'm able to interact with them." Quoted in August 2017, *AOPA Pilot-Turbine Edition*, "Life on the fly: A corporate pilot's many hats," by Sylvia Schneider Horne. At only age 20, Laura decided to pursue an aviation career. She built her corporate business with a strong customer service base. In 2014, she also became a member of the "around the world in about 80 days" club. Well, in only 78 days, Azara landed in 29 countries and 35 airports in her unmodified Pilatus PC-12NG, flying about 27,500 miles. Back at her aviation job as a corporate pilot, she handles baggage, people, airport services, and sometimes stocks the pantry so it is not all glamorous with a leather flight jacket and aviator sun glasses. Laura Azara likes that the days are all different and corporate pilot is a good fit for now.

Banglesdorf, Rene

"Do not undervalue yourself. Don't underestimate what you bring to the table as a woman or a business person. Women have certain nurturing, multitasking, and customer-service oriented skills that are totally foreign to men. Don't bury those. Use them to your advantage." Quoted on www.mscareergirl.com. Rene is co-founder of Charlie Bravo Aviation in Austin, Texas. Her company assists with the purchase, selling, and leasing of corporate aircraft worldwide. High tech and high touch have made her team successful. As one of the few women owners, Rene also encourages other female leaders through the International Aviation Women's Association. She serves on their Advisory Board. In 2020, this dynamic aviation leader was named by the U.S. Secretary of Transportation, Elaine Chao, to join the new federally-mandated DOT Women in Aviation Advisory Board. WIAAB only has 30 members whose two-year mission is to develop strategies to recommend solutions to the President and Congress to increase women in the aviation industry. Rene is also active in the National Business Aircraft Association and the National Air Transportation Association. In 2016, she co-authored the leadership book, *Crushing Mediocrity*. In 2019, she published *Stand Up: How to Flourish When the Odds are Stacked Against You.*

Barnes, Geveva "Gennie" B.

"I was just worn out. And when we got home, I didn't even unpack my bags. I just sat down in a reclining chair and sat there all night long, because your adrenalin, you know, the whole time you're traveling, you're pumped up. You really can't sleep well, because you're afraid you're going to miss your wake-up call, afraid you'll miss the plane. And all of a sudden, everything is down. You don't have to wake up at a certain time the next morning. You don't have to pack a bag to put out in the hall." Quoted from her March 26, 1999, NASA Oral History Project recording about the worldwide post-Apollo mission tour she helped manage. In 1962, Gennie began her NASA career as a secretary at the Headquarters. A year later, she joined NASA Public Affairs in a secretarial role with "additional behind-the-scenes" duties for special events and ceremonies. Even with three small children, she coordinated Astronaut appearances, prepared briefing books, and responded to fan-mail. Gennie became a public affairs assistant for Neil Armstrong. She retired in 1994. Her story reminds me of the T-shirt printed with "Do You Want to Talk to the Man-in-Charge, OR, the Women Who Actually Knows What is Going On?"

Barrett, Heidi

"I've loved them my whole life. There's something magic about a helicopter. It's very 3-D-a complete magic carpet thing that you can't get any other way." Quoted in August 2012, *EAA Sport Aviation Magazine*, "Heidi's Helicopter," by Lane Wallace. As a very successful career woman, one of our leading Napa winemakers, Heidi spent 25 years crafting some world-class wines. Married to a pilot, Bo Barrett, Heidi was busy with her career and raising two children. Aviation was low in her needs state back then. In her late 40s, what seemed like another "mid-life crisis" story, actually was the fulfillment of her life-long dream of flying a helicopter. Not only did it create Gestalt with her dream, the mobility of a helicopter in business, especially the wine business, proved Heidi made yet another stellar decision. Now, Heidi Barrett not only owns and flies her own helicopter, but she has her own landing pad at her Napa Valley home. Her story reminds me of the T-shirt printed with, "Awesome Copter Pilot Living The Dream."

Bartell, Shana

"I dream often of the life this will give my family. I look to inspire my children, my little sister, other students, and single mothers by showing them that with enough work, you can make incredible things happen." Quoted in January 2, 2019 *General Aviation News* story, "Single mom of five pursues her dream to become a pilot." Shana is also pursuing her airframe and powerplant (A & P) mechanic certificate at Southern Utah University. She continues to pursue a private pilot certificate, as well.

Bass, Beverley
"After my first lesson, I came home and told my parents that I would fly for the rest of my life." Quoted in March 19, 2016/updated July 7, 2017 *The News-Press,* "Fort Myers Native Beverley Bass Made Aviation History" by Cynthia A. Williams. www.news-press.com. At 24 years old, Bass joined American Airlines as a flight engineer. Later, moving up to First Officer. In 1978, Beverley became a Charter Member of the International Society of Women Airline Pilots (ISA+21). In 1986, she broke the glass ceiling at American Airlines becoming their first female Captain. In 1999, Beverley Bass became the first woman to Captain a B-777 in an airline operation. In 2008, Captain Bass retired from American. Today, an award-winning musical, "Come From Away," celebrates the story of the people of Gander, Newfoundland, welcoming the crews and passengers grounded by the 9/11/2001 terrorists' attacks. Bass was one of those airline pilots. Currently, Jenn Colella plays the intrepid Captain Beverley Bass in the stage production.

Beaver, Marge
"[I] got addicted pretty quickly. Probably on the first flight." Quoted in February 2012 *EAA Sport Aviation Magazine,* "Eye on the World Marge Beaver's Aerial Art," by Lane Wallace. As one of our premiere aerial photographers, Marge has captured the natural beauty in nearly every state. Her aerial art photographs have graced the covers of over 35 books and magazines. Her EAA Oshkosh aerial posters were top sellers for years. After raising her family, she discovered a new passion. She began flight training in her mid-40s. She earned her instrument rating in a tailwheel. Soon, her thriving business required her to retrofit a plane for that perfect photograph seen with an artist eye. A Cessna Cardinal was what she needed. Marge has flown about 7,000 hours in her flying studio, with a focus on the Great Lakes and Michigan landscape. This

"late bloomer" has created three aerial art books, *Above The North*, *Above the Lighthouses-Lake Michigan*, and *Above West Michigan: Aerial Photography of West Michigan*. Marge Beaver, pilot-artist, mixes a perfect blend of air and art.

Beech, Olive Ann

"I like to have around me people who find ways to do things, not tell me why they can't be done." In 1932, she co-founded Beech Aircraft Corporation with her husband. Often described in our aviation history as the "First Lady of Aviation," Olive Beech was a dynamic aerospace businesswoman. A savvy marketer and financial manager, she helped Beech grow into a premier brand. In 1950, after her husband's death, Olive worked tirelessly with employees, Beech Aircraft dealers, and owners to insure the strength of the company and quality of the brand. America in the 1950s was in post-war prosperity. But, the popular culture was "Father Knows Best." For Olive Beech to win acceptance as an industry leader and be so successful was quite remarkable. In 1973, she was inducted into the National Aviation Hall of Fame, along with many other awards and recognitions over her lifetime.

Beeler, MayCay

"Take a gal flying! Cheer her on! Share the magic aloft. Spread your contagious enthusiasm! Let her know anything is possible, and any dream is attainable if she is willing to work for it!" Quoted in the May 1, 2015 Airplanista blog www.av8rdan.com by Dan Pimentel. MayCay (a family nickname for the more formal Mary Catherine) is a highly qualified pilot and Certified Flight Instructor with a passion for promoting aviation. She is a veteran broadcast personality, award-winning author, and a record-setting pilot. MayCay created "The Diva flight experience" to empower women through aviation. Learn more www.Divaflight.com.

(MayCay Beeler. Courtesy photograph MayCay Beeler)

Berwyn, Cyndhi

"Credibility is extremely important, and I believe that comes from being honest and competent, but also [from] being accountable. Once you become known for delivering a consistent, strong performance, the personal biases evaporate, and you become trusted. This is a career field where it is extremely evident that you did your work to prepare because you can't fake it as a professional pilot." Quoted in April 2020 *Flying* magazine, "Cyndhi Berwyn From the Air Force to Flying Hospital," by Dan Pimentel. In the 1970s, Cyndhi flew gliders while studying meteorology at the University of Hawaii. In her senior year, the Air Force opened up for women to fly. She competed and was selected as one of the first women in that program. Later, she became an Air Force Instructor in the T-37 and T-38. All the while, Berwyn continued to build her aviation creds by flying hot air balloons, seaplanes, and helicopters. When her active duty ended, she joined the Air Force Reserve flying KC-10s. She also joined Fed Ex where she has flown for the past 34 years. On the FedEx aviation team, Cyndhi has been a flight engineer, first officer, and Captain on the Boeing 727, Douglas DC-10, Airbus A-300, McDonnell Douglas MD-11, and Boeing 777. In short, this gal knows how to fly. But wait, there is more. In her off-duty hours she is the Captain of the Orbis International Flying Eye Hospital, a one-of-a-kind McDonnell Douglas MD-10-30 that travels around the world bringing much needed medical training to doctors and vision-saving treatments to underserved people in Panama, the United Arab Emirates, India, Ethiopia, Chile, Peru, and Jamaica. Inside the plane is a full surgical hospital. It takes a well-trained team to transition from "flight" mode to "hospital"…and back. What a gift to the world through aviation and outstanding pilots as Captain Cyndhi Berwyn.

Bierman, Elizabeth

"If you are passionate about something and want to make a difference, I promise there is a way to do that with engineering. Engineers solve problems, period. They think of new ideas and bring them to fruition. For those aspiring to be engineers, build a community of support." Quoted December 14, 2014, *Lifehacker.com/career-spotlight,* "What I Do as an Aerospace Engineer," by Andy Orin. Elizabeth specializes in avionics and is a senior project engineer at Honeywell Aerospace. She is in the leadership of the Society of Women Engineers which helps women with networking and mutual career support.

Biss, Emily

"To get the job you want, be the best at the job you have." Quoted in October/November 2011, *99 News* magazine, "Emily Biss: Combining What See Loves," by Julia Reiners. Emily is an Ivy League-educated engineer who wanted to blend her technical skills with her passion for flying. She formulated a plan that would bridge where she was to where she wanted to be. She also took stock of the additional skill set she needed. In 2001, she began flight instructing and maintenance test piloting. Working to be her best, she finally landed at Boeing as a test pilot and demonstration flight pilot for potential 737 customers. Recently, she was accepted as a new member of the Society of Experimental Test Pilots.

Brame, Tiffany

"When pilots would come in with this or that problem or scenario, sometimes the other mechanics would have no idea what they were talking about. I just understand what pilots need and look for and what they're likely to notice. I think it's really beneficial and makes me a better mechanic." Quoted in the summer 2020 *Mission Aviation Flight Watch*, "Ministry Spotlight." Tiffany is a new aviation maintenance specialist. Soon, she will be serving other Mission Aviation Fellowship pilots. As a pilot and, now aircraft mechanic, Tiffany easily "speaks pilot." Brame hails from Michigan. Even before she finished high school, she felt a clear calling to serve overseas and expand the Gospel. During her aviation training and working as a mechanic, short-term mission trips confirmed her belief. Serving soon in Jakarta, Indonesia, Tiffany will help maintain Mission Aviation Fellowship planes, serving the region with 260,000,000 souls. Learn more www.MAF.org.

Broadwick, Georgia "Tiny"
"I tell you, honey, it was the most wonderful sensation in the world!" Quoted in a March 12, 2015, Smithsonian Air and Space Museum story about her donating her silk parachute in 1964 to the Smithsonian. See https://airandspace.si.edu/stories/editorial/georgia-%E2%80%9Ctiny%E2%80%9D-broadwick%E2%80%99s-parachute. As early as 1908, Tiny, billed as "The Doll Girl," in ruffled bloomers, silk dress, ribbons in her hair, wearing a bonnet, and only 15 years old, became our first woman to parachute. "Tiny" was only three pounds at birth, but her nickname stuck because as a popular air show performer she only weighed around 80 pounds and was very petite. Tiny Broadwick was a very popular performer and aviation pioneer.

Brown, Tahirah Lamont
"The biggest obstacle in front of you is yourself. Knowing who you are is essential. By doing so, you can better focus on attaining what you want in life." Quoted in May/June 2018 WAI *Aviation For Women* magazine, "The Power of Self-Awareness," by Michael Bielskis. In 2002, Tahirah was hired as the first African American female pilot at FedEx. Now, Captain Tahirah is a testament to persistence and networking. Along the way, many mentored and encouraged her. She recommends joining associations and attending conferences to meet

industry leaders. Tahirah's career was assisted by joining The Organization of Black Aerospace Professionals (OBAP). Often scholarship and training opportunities are available to students and members.

Bundchen, Gisele

"The more you trust your intuition, the more empowered you become, the stronger you become, and the happier you become." Quote in July 20, 2014, www.Bustle.com "Quotes of Model Wisdom from Gisele on Her Birthday," by Arielle Dachille. In 2009, supermodel Gisele earned her helicopter rating. While seven months pregnant, it was challenging to learn the skills to master all the controls. Her main motivation, in addition to safety when her family flew, was to fully understand the "nuts and bolts" of the chopper. She served as the UN Environmental Goodwill Ambassador to find alternative sources for jet fuel. In 1999, at age 19, the Brazilian model flew into super stardom as a Victoria Secret Angel. In 2006, she retired those feathered wings to earn her helicopter pilot wings.

Burrow, Sarah Deal

"Nobody wanted me assigned to them. I found this out years later. Finally the commanding officer of my first unit said, 'Is she a qualified pilot? I don't care if it's a man or a woman, send her this way'… Be strong. Do your job. Don't expect anything special. And…know who your friends are." Quoted in Shannon Huffman Polson's new book, *The Grit Factor*. Sarah earned her single and multi-engine commercial flight certificates while still in college. She competed on the Kent State Precision Flight team. In 1992, she joined the Marine Corps. In 1993, when aviation slots opened up for women, she boldly asked to be considered. She was the first female Marine selected for Naval Aviation training. In 1995, she became the Marine Corps first woman aviator qualified for the rotary wing CH-53E.

3

C-Charlie to D-Delta

In life you are either a passenger or the pilot.
It is your choice. ~ Unknown

Caputo, Bonnie Tiburzi

"Airline flying was traditionally a macho job, sought after by the guys with the right stuff and a particular kind of cool swagger. Those attributes may be reassuring, but coordination, training, and a fierce desire to do the job as well as it can be done are far more important than male muscles." Written by Captain Bonnie in her chapter, "In a Place Called the Cockpit," in *Women Who Fly: True Stories by Women Airline Pilots*. At age 19, Bonnie earned her private ticket and continued to earn advanced ratings. In addition to charter operations, she conducted flight instruction. By 1973, at age 24, American Airlines hired her as their first woman flight engineer. She became the first woman in the world to earn a Flight Engineer Turbo-jet Aircraft rating. Retiring in 1999, after a 26 year career at American as a Captain having flown the Boeing 727, 757 and 767 in the fleet. Her autobiography, *Takeoff: The Story of America's First Woman Pilot For A Major Airline,* shares her aviation career journey. In 2018, she was inducted into the Women in Aviation International Pioneer Hall of Fame.

Cavagnaro, Catherine

"Don't wait like I did! If you are resourceful, there are ways to make your aviation dream happen. Start by visiting your local airport and let your interests be known. The aviation community is generous and loves to support those with a passion for flight." Quoted March 2019, *Flight Training*, "Catherine Cavagnaro: Spin Aficionado." Dr. Cavagnaro is now widely known as an expert on spins, aerobatics, and upset recovery techniques. She has made up for the time during her earlier years when flying was out of her reach because of cost. As they often say, "Better Late than Never!" Sometimes life just gets in the way of our dreams until we can break out into the endless possibilities in aviation. Now the Chief…and only Flight Instructor at the Sewanee-Franklin Airport Ace Aerobatic School, mathematics professor Cavagnaro is well known on campus and across the United States for her knowledge and skill. Her trusty 1979 Cessna Aerobat is called "Wilbur." Catherine Elizabeth Cavagnaro was named the 2018 National Safety Representative of the Year by the Federal Aviation Administration. The same year she was inducted into the Tennessee Aviation Hall of Fame.

Chabrian, Peggy

"It is an exciting time to be a young woman in the field of aviation and space. The doors are open and the needs are great. Airlines are looking for qualified pilots, manufacturers are looking for bright engineers, airplane owners are looking for talented mechanics, and companies need passionate individuals to keep it all running." Writing in the 2019 *Women in Aviation International Aviation for Girls* magazine. Dr. Chabrian is the founder of WAI. She is a highly-rated aviator with commercial, instrument, multi-engine, flight instructor, seaplane, and helicopter ratings. She has earned numerous awards and held prestigious academic and leadership positions. Recently she retired from the WAI presidency.

Chance, Mary Van Scyoc

"I was privileged to fly much of my life. I was so fortunate to have had parents who allowed me to pursue my dreams. I was lucky to have married a man who shared my dreams and to have had children who supported all my endeavors." From Mary's book, *A Lifetime of*

Chances. By chance, Mary saw a newspaper ad during World War II announcing women were welcome to apply for air traffic control. The only requirements were a college degree and a pilot's license. Mary had both. On June 1, 1942, Mary headed to Denver, Colorado. Mary is often considered the very first civilian woman to become an air traffic controller. She had a long and storied career in aviation and Air Traffic Control (ATC).

Chao, Elaine

"Don't be afraid to try new things! If you're interested in aviation, take flying lessons. See how you like it. Flying is an incredible experience, and you'll meet a lot of great female role models!" Quoted in November/December 2019 *WAI Aviation For Women* magazine, "10 Questions For U.S. Secretary of Transportation, Elaine Chao," by Kelly Murphy.

(DOT Secretary Elaine Chao at Kentucky's historic Bowman Field.)

Born in Taipei, Elaine Chao, migrated with her parents to the U.S. at age eight. By age 19, she had become a citizen. Years of higher education at Mount Holyoke, Dartmouth, and Harvard Business School, provided a strong administrative skill set. In 2017, she was appointed U.S. Secretary of Transportation. She is the first Asian American (Chinese) woman in U.S. history to be appointed to a President's cabinet, not once but twice. From 2001-09, Chao also served as Secretary of Labor, a cabinet level position.

Chawla, Kalpana
"The journey matters as much as the goal." Born in India, she broke barriers as a woman in that country earning her degree in aeronautical engineering. In 1984, she earned her University of Texas master's in aerospace engineering. In 1988, her career began at NASA Ames Research Center. In 1991, Chawla became a naturalized citizen of the United States. Along the way, Kalpana had also earned advanced ratings in airplanes, gliders, seaplanes, with Commercial and multi-engine licenses. She was a Certified Flight Instructor for airplanes and gliders. She applied to join our Astronaut Corps. By 1997, Kalpana became the first Indian American astronaut and first Indian woman in space as a NASA mission specialist on Space Shuttle Columbia. In 2003, on her second space mission STS-107, Chawla and her Space Shuttle Columbia crew members were all tragically killed seconds after lift-off.

The big difference between a pilot and an aviator is one is a technician; the other is an artist in love with flight. ~Unknown

(NASA Kalpana Chawla. Courtesy NASA)

Chung, Stephanie

"We as women are gifted in so many ways and it's important that we focus on our talents, strengthen our gifts, and support and encourage others along the way." From Stephanie's book, *Profit Like A Girl.* Recently Chung was named president of JetSuite, making Stephanie the first African American president of a private aviation company. She has a 30-plus-year career in customer service and sales. She began as an airline ramp agent before moving to airline customer service and sales so she literally knows the back and the front ends of aviation service. In April 2020, COVID forced JetSuite to halt operation and furlough crews. As an adapter to change, keep up with Stephanie at her personal web site www.StephanieChung.com.

Clark, Julie

"I removed my resume photo and wrote down my name as Julian. Also, there's that box that says, 'Sex: F or M?' It's always a little, teeny square. I'd just skip it, like I hadn't seen it. I just wanted them to call me. Nobody would call me, and if I called them, they'd hang up on me.

It was very discouraging." Quoted in March 1, 2007, *Airports Journal*, "Julie Clark: From Flight Attendant to Captain to Aerobatics Superstar." Julie faced early gender discrimination in the airline industry. But, in 1976, Golden West Airline hired her. In 2003, Clark retired as an airline Captain. During those years, she also became a beloved solo aerobatics pilot and air show performer. In November 2019, in her final air show performance, Julie Clark again mesmerized the crowd with her signature aerobatic ballet choreographed with red, white and blue smoke to Lee Greenwood's patriotic song, "God Bless the USA." She is a Charter Member of the International Society of Women Airline Pilots-ISA+21.

Cleave, Mary L.
"My interest is space and aviation was developed early with an interest in science fiction and model airplanes. In middle school, my science fair entry was an astronomy demonstration and my flying lessons started at 14 years old." Dr. Cleave is quoted in *Colorado's Astronauts: In Their Own Words.* She is an engineer and former NASA Deputy Associate Administrator.

Coleman, Bessie
"I refused to take no for an answer." Published December 10, 2019 by Norbert Juma at https://everydaypower.com/bessie-coleman-quotes/. In 1921, Bessie became the world's first licensed civilian African American pilot. She left her Chicago business for France to receive her flight training because she was refused flight instruction in her home country. Returning to America to much fanfare, Coleman toured the country barnstorming as "Brave Bessie," raising money for her dream of an African American flying school. She was also called "Queen Bess" because she "ruled" the sky. Bessie would only perform if the crowds were desegregated and entered through the same gates, which was a rarity in some locations. On April 20, 1926, Coleman was thrown from a Curtiss JN-4 at 2,000 feet flown by her mechanic, William D. Wills, in preparation for an air show performance. Bessie died instantly

upon impact with the ground. Willis died in the plane crash. It was later discovered that a wrench used to service the engine slid into the gearbox and jammed it. Bessie was 34 years old. In 1995, Coleman was inducted into the Women in Aviation International Pioneer Hall of Fame. In 2006, The National Aviation Hall of Fame inducted this aviation legend.

(Queen Bessie. Courtesy of Library of Congress archive)

Coleman, Catherine Grace "Cady"

"When Sally Ride made her first flight, after, right after that she came to MIT and she talked to the women students, and I just looked at her and I thought, I want that job. And you never actually think that you will get selected for that job, but here, she was somebody that it seemed to count that she was educated and that she really liked learning as much as she could about things that she was passionate about, and so she was a scientist and at the same time she was also, somebody that was helping to explore the universe, and she got to fly jets, scuba dive, all these things that I loved, and I was actually just so inspired to meet her and it made a big difference to me to have met her that day. She doesn't remember meeting me—we've talked about it since—but for me it was significant because I'd seen a lot of astronauts on TV, in pictures; none of them looked like me. It was a bunch of guys that seemed a lot older to me and they didn't have much hair, and it just didn't really make me think, that could be me, and then I meet somebody like Sally Ride and I think, maybe that could be me." Quoted in October 28, 2018, NASA preflight interview. Coleman is a veteran of two Space Shuttle Missions and a six-month mission on the International Space Station. She is a scientist, STEM advocate, former U.S. Air Force officer, and now retired astronaut.

Collins, Eileen

"Flying gave me a purpose. It also gave me a sense of freedom, independence, and the satisfaction of seeing results from hard work and practice. And, of course, I enjoy the beautiful view from above." Quoted in March/April 2020, *Aviation for Women* magazine, "Second Wind: A conversation with Eileen Collins, NASA Astronaut, first female space shuttle pilot and commander," by Kelly Murphy. Retired Air Force Colonel Collins is a former military flight instructor and test pilot. In 1995, Astronaut Collins became our first woman to pilot a Space Shuttle Mission-SYS-63. In 1999, she became our first woman to command a Space Shuttle Mission-STS-93. In 2005, she again commanded NASA STS-114 mission. Eileen Collins is a member of the Women in Aviation International Pioneer Hall of Fame. In 2009, she was inducted into the National Aviation Hall of Fame.

Cornwell, Patricia

"The first time I flew solo, my knees were knocking together-literally-I had to start singing to myself. Then all of a sudden it was like, 'Oh my God, this is the most fun thing I have ever done. I am flying. I'm alone and it's just me doing this.'" Best-selling author quoted October 10, 2015 in *The Guardian,* "Patricia Cornwell: How extreme Sports changed my Life." For authenticity in her highly-acclaimed crime thrillers. Cornwell took to the sky because the tech-savvy niece, Lucy, of her forensic sleuth, Dr. Kay Scarpetta, is a helicopter pilot. Cornwell's novels have been translated into 36 languages and have been selling for decades, along with a long list of fact-based books. Research started her helicopter experience. She has owned four. Now, Patricia Cornwell tells people she's rather have a helicopter than a diamond ring!

Cox, Jessica

"Never let fear stand in the way of an opportunity." From her inspirational book, *Disarm Your Limits: The Flight Formula to Lift You to Success and Propel You to the Next Horizon.* What a blessing to our world. This young woman is the world's first licensed armless pilot. Because of a rare birth defect, Jessica was born without arms. She learned to use her feet as hands. In 2005, after earning her degree from the University of Arizona, Cox, with an Able Flight scholarship, began her quest to fly. In October 2008, at age 25, after three years of flight training, Jessica earned her Sport Pilot Certificate. Cox also is the first armless person to earn a black-belt in the American Taekwondo Association. She is, a certified scuba diver, and extraordinary motivational speaker. A documentary about her exceptional life is called *Right Footed.*

Cristoforetti, Samantha

"…I'm appreciative of the fact that I'm in a position of being a role model. So I just try to be myself and show that there are things that you can do, that they are an option, and then a young girl, young women, can take from it whatever they need and it's useful for them." Quoted in May 14, 2017 The Verge.com, "Astronaut Samantha Cristoforetti on tweeting from space and brewing the first zero-G espresso," by Alessandra Potenza. Cristoforetti, Italy's first woman in space, is an Italian European Space Agency astronaut (2009), former Italian Air Force pilot, and an engineer. She logged 119 days and 16 hours in space and held the record for the longest single space flight by a woman until June 2017 when American astronaut, Peggy Whitson, surpassed that milestone. As a foreign exchange student in high school, Samantha landed in the United States and was able to attend a space camp. Returning to Europe, she earned advanced degrees. As part of her training with the Italian Air Force, she logged over 500 hours in six types of military aircraft. Fluent in Italian, English, German, French, and Russian, she is learning Chinese. In 2019, Cristoforetti commanded a NEEMO mission on the seafloor testing technologies for a deep space mission and lunar explorations.

(Astronaut Samantha Cristoforetti. Courtesy ESA/NASA)

Culver, Chrissi

"My advice for anyone looking to start a career in air traffic control is to be eager. Be eager to learn, be eager to do something different, and be eager to help those coming behind you. While the job can be demanding of your time and energy, it is also very rewarding and one that I wouldn't trade for any other in the world." Chrissi wrote this advice in the July-August 2020, WAI *Aviation for Women* magazine in her own words, "Organizer of the Sky." As an air traffic control specialist at Fort Worth Air Route Traffic Control Center (ARTCC), Culver assists pilots climbing and descending, and sequences airplanes for landing in a complicated Dallas-Fort Worth air space. Her description of her daily "routine" reminds me of the T-shirt. "Female Air Traffic Controller-Multi-tasking Problem Solver!"

Custodio, Olga

"My mantra is *'Querer es poder.'* (Where there's a will there's a way). I believe everyone has the potential to do it. They just have to believe in themselves enough to actually do it." Quoted from May 28, 2012, *Daily Mail Reporter,* "When I was told to List the Three Jobs I wanted, I said 'pilot, pilot, pilot:' Meet the First Latina To Fly Planes for the U.S. Military." In 1980, Custodio became the first Latina U.S. Air Force pilot. Later, at American Airlines, she became their first Latina pilot. In 2008, she retired as Captain Custodio.

Damato, Joanne "Jo"

"I've been passionate about aviation my whole life. I was that 15-year-old high schooler inspired by the idea of a career in aviation, but it was a challenge for my parents, teachers, and guidance counselors to help me start that journey." Quoted in July 28, 2020 *State Aviation Journal Skybrief,* "NBAA's Damato Joined DOT Task Force Focused on Youth Access to Aviation Careers," by Kim Stevens. In 2019, Damato became Vice President of Educational Strategy and Workforce Development at the National Business Aviation Association (NBAA.). In 2001, she joined the NBAA team serving in several key staff and leadership positions. She is a Certified Flight Instructor, holding single and multi-engine land instrument ratings, and a commercial pilot certificate. Jo Damato is a Florida Institute of Technology graduate and also earned a Master's in Aeronautical Science from Embry-Riddle Aeronautical University.

Deen, Taylor

"Keep all your doors open. Your career direction will change several times and you should let it. If you are too focused on one path you may miss out on another path that's an amazing adventure." Quoted in April 2017, *Flight Training,* "Taylor Deen: Blimp Pilot." As the senior pilot for the famous Goodyear Blimp, Taylor has flown the airship for five years. An experienced pilot before joining the airship in 2005 Deen earned her pilot certificate. Then, came the exciting and challenging flying as an Alaska bush pilot. Machines, weather and people are all thrown at you in remote locations so your quickly become a problem-solver and learn from others. Before she joined the Goodyear flight team, Taylor had flown 2,500 fixed wing hours. Now, she has over 2,000 airship hours. In addition to understanding the special nature of flying this iconic blimp, the Goodyear team are ambassadors for the company and for the unique passenger experience of seeing the world at the slower speed of usually 30 mph. Big grins are often the result.

Dellion, Camilla
"My best advice to someone who wants to start flying is to push yourself out of your comfort zone. Let your learning process take the time it needs. And remember everyone can fly a drone." Words in her video at www.womenwhodrone.co as Brand Ambassador for The Maldives.

Drewry, Faith
"At no point in my training did I feel like being a woman was going to hold me back at all. I just loved to fly and nothing could have stopped me." Quote in the February/March 2014, *Tallahassee Woman*, "Women Take Flight!" by Heather Thomas. At age 14, following the aviation path set by her aunt, Faith started training. At age 22, she bought her own airplane. Now, as co-owner of FL Aviation Center with Lacey Smith, nestled in renovated space at Tallahassee Regional airport. They have a growing fleet of training planes and a team of flight instructors. The mission statement for FL Aviation Center is to create, nurture, and inspire a new generation of pilots to become passionate, life-long ambassadors to ensure the future of General Aviation.

Duckworth, Ladda Tammy
"I never set out to be the first in anything, and with a lot of these 'firsts,' it really makes me wonder how it's taken so long." Quoted in April 16, 2018 *Fortune The Broadsheet*. In 2004, Tammy Duckworth was the pilot of a Black Hawk UH-60 that was hit by a rocket-propelled grenade

shot by Iraqi terrorists. Badly wounded, both her legs were amputated. After a long recovery, she provided leadership in Illinois and at the federal government level in Veterans Affairs. In 2011, Tammy Duckworth was inducted into the WAI Pioneer Hall of Fame. In 2012, Duckworth became the first disabled woman elected to Congress. She also became the first Thai American woman elected from Illinois. In 2016, she was elected to the U.S. Senate where later she became our first woman to give birth while serving in the Senate. In 2018, she received the International Ninety-Nines Award of Inspiration.

Duffy, Genesah
"I stopped at St. Pete-Clearwater Airport one day and took a discovery flight. We flew over Clearwater Beach and Tampa Bay in a Cessna 172, and that was it. I knew right then I wanted to be a pilot, even though I didn't know any pilots and no one in my family flew." Quoted in May 1, 2020, *AOPA Pilot* story by Dave Hirschman www.aopa.org/news-and-media/all-news/2020/may/pilot/pilots-genesah-duffy. Genesah has flown her way to advanced ratings, including multi-engine and seaplanes. She is a Certified Flight Instructor and manager of flight operations for ICON Aircraft in Florida. The two-seat ICON A5 amphibian offers versatility. In 2019, Genesah was filmed in California during a demonstration flight with entertainer, Jay Leno, on his popular series, "Jay Leno's Garage."

Dunbar, Bonnie J.
"My father taught my siblings and me how to dream. Our parents taught us that it didn't matter what we did as long as we tried, picked ourselves up from failure, and were good citizens." Quoted in *Gutsy Girls Go for Science*. Dr. Dunbar earned her Bachelor's and Master's in ceramic engineering and a private pilot license. She held important research and engineering positions at Boeing Company, Harwell Laboratory Atomic Energy Research Establishment, and Rockwell International. In 1978, she joined NASA as a flight controller. In 1980, Dunbar was selected as a mission specialist astronaut. Our seventh American woman in space,

by now Dr. Dunbar, became a veteran of five space missions and has traveled 20-plus million miles on Atlantis, Challenger, Columbia and Endeavor. In 1994, she even trained in Star City with Russian Cosmonauts. After providing NASA leadership as Associate Director of Technical Integration and Risk Management at Johnson Space Center and Life Science Directorate, Dr. Bonnie Dunbar retired to become the President of the Museum of Flight. In 2010, she returned to academic positions at University of Houston, and later Texas A&M. Bonnie Dunbar's accomplishments remind me of what Amelia Earhart said, "Everyone has oceans to fly, if they have the heart to do it. Is it reckless? Maybe. But what do dreams know of boundaries?"

(Air Force archival 1944 photograph of L-R WASP Frances Green, Margaret "Peg" Kirchner, Ann Waldner and Blanche Osborn on a ferry training mission at Lockbourne Army Airfield, Ohio, leaving their B-17 Flying Fortress called "Pistol Packin' Mama)

4
E-Echo to I-India

Believe in your infinite possibilities. ~ Unknown

Earhart, Amelia Mary "A.E."

(Amelia Earhart. Library of Congress archival photo)

"It doesn't take any more prowess to be a super-flyer than it does to be a super something else." Quoted in *The Quotable Amelia Earhart* by Michele Wehrwein Albion. Earhart is one of the most famous pilots of all time. She was the 16th woman to earn a pilot license. On November 2, 1929, she provided significant direction and leadership in the founding of the Ninety-Nines for women aviators. On May 20, 1932, she became the first woman to fly solo across the Atlantic. On July 2, 1937, during an attempt to circumnavigate the globe, Earhart and her Lockheed Electra Model 10-E disappeared over the Pacific Ocean. In 1968, the National Aviation Hall of Fame enshrined her. In 1996, she became a member of the Women in Aviation International Pioneer Hall of Fame.

Eddy, Vivian Cadman
"Well, you won't hire me as a pilot." Vivian candidly answered the American Airlines interviewer about why she was applying to be a stewardess as reported in the February 2008 *AOPA Pilot* magazine, "Gallery of Legends," by Alton K. Marsh. In 1930, at age nine, Vivian's passion for flying began when she witnessed an airshow. By age 19, she was already licensed to fly airplanes. In 1943, 22-year-old Vivian joined the WASP class 43-W-5. As a WASP, she ferried aircraft from the factories to locations where they were shipped overseas. She was in the WASP Ferry Command stationed at Love Field in Dallas and Palm Springs Army Air Base. She was an Ops officer who flew P-51 Mustangs, her favorite. She flew eight from the Los Angeles factory across America to Newark, New Jersey. She also flew many other military aircraft. When the WASP were sent home, Vivian felt her place was still in the air, even if it meant she would be in the back of the airplane as a stewardess. But, with all her DC-3 flight experience, she was always invited by the American Airlines flight crews to join them in the cockpit and take the controls once again.

Flannigan, Meagan

"I think my first message first and foremost for anything you want to do regardless of if you're a girl or a boy…you just dream big and you go for it. A friend of mine said, '…if you want something bad enough with your heart, you figure out a way to make it happen with your brain.' That's what I did and that's what a lot of my friends have done." Quoted in November 2017, *EAA eHotline*, "Navy Fighter Pilot Meagan Flannigan to be Featured in Museum Speaker Series," by Sam Oleson. In 1986, as a ten-year-old, the iconic film, *Top Gun*, made a huge impression on her. Her goal became to grow up and be a fighter pilot. She knew she would have to work hard and keep her dream alive. Little did she know, women were excluded by the Navy at that time. If her parents knew, they never told her so Meagan kept setting her goals for "fighter pilot" success. In 1991, Congress lifted the ban on women flying in combat aircraft. Timing is everything sometimes. As a U.S. Naval Academy cadet, Flannigan set her sights on flight school which became a reality. Then, miracle of miracle, she was one of the last four pilots selected for the Grumman F-14 Tomcat, the very same type of jet featured in *Top Gun* which had inspired the whole journey. She said, "On that first flight I knew it was worth it." In 2005-06, Meagan flew the Tomcat from the *USS Theodore Roosevelt* during the Iraq War. When the Navy retired the Tomcat from service, Flannigan transitioned to the F/A-18F Super Hornet. She has logged more than 1,250 hours in fighter jet aircraft. The short-term sacrifices she made to achieve her life-long dream proved women are successful in the face of what appears to some to be overwhelming odds. Be the gal who decides to go for it!

Fleming, Darlene

"Aviation offers unique opportunities for women. If you enjoy travel, pursuing training as a flight attendant gives you great skills which will benefit you for the rest of your life. Flight attendants must be extremely organized, have super people skills, and understand team work. You can work your way up to supervisory positions which add to your career opportunities within that company and other aviation and aerospace jobs. Traveling broadens your understanding of the world and business. As you gain in seniority, you can juggle your work schedule to accommodate your family needs. If being home at night with your family is important, you can always make a lateral move within your company to gate service or other important positions within aviation." Darlene Fleming, former International Pan Am Stewardess (1969-1974). By the end of the 1970s, "flight attendant" replaced 'Stewardess." More recently, some use "Cabin Crew" or "Cabin Staff."

Fox, Kathy
"Pursue your dreams but realize your life path may take you in a different direction. Be flexible. You might end up in a better place than you ever dreamed of." Quoted in November/December 2018 *Ninety-Nines* magazine, "Kathy Fox," by Jann Clark. Kathy's childhood dream was to be an astronaut. But a financial forced choice sent her to McGill University but science and math would be her focus to be used as a possible stepping stone to space. During those collegiate years, skydiving became a substitute to be in the air at an affordable cost. She was soon elected president of the Canadian Sport Parachuting Association. Then, in 1976, she seized the aviation opportunity with Transport Canada as a licensed Air Controller. Still not a pilot, at least Kathy was still at the airport and she could tell pilots where to fly. Finally, in 1978, Kathy earned her private pilot license. Joining a flying club, she built time and training to acquire her commercial license and flight instructor, multi-engine, and IFR ratings. She added airline transport license. Talk about unleased pent-up desire. Wow. Not satisfied with all the accomplishments, Kathy Fox opened a flight school, charter operation, and aviation maintenance center. Oh, she earned her MA in Business Administration all while continuing her ATC job. In 1996, Fox transferred from ATC to Nav Canada, a privately run, not-for-profit enterprise which owns and operates Canada's civil air navigation system. She worked her way to Vice-President. In 2007, she announced her retirement. But, the next day she joined the

Transportation Safety Board of Canada in only a part-time capacity. By 2014, and again in 2018, Kathy Fox was elected Chair. Over her long aviation career, Kathy was inducted into several Air and Space Halls of Fame and the WAI Pioneer Hall of Fame. Sky Star Kathy Fox has followed her own sage career advice.

Gaffaney, Mary

"I always had to use both hands to snap the old Stearman, so the first Pitts I flew, Zoom! Zoom! They said it was a beautiful double snap. I had to tell them I only meant one. It's so easy to fly. Point it, it goes; pull it, it snaps! Bang! Bang! Oh, it's fun." Quoted in the 1972 *Sport Aerobatics* magazine describing her award-winning aerobatic performances in her black and yellow 180hp Pitts Special. In the 1940s, Mary began flying at age 16. She loved the freedom in the air. Gaffaney became the first U.S. female skywriter. She became the first female helicopter pilot in Florida. In 1970, Mary became the first American to win a gold medal in world aerobatic competition. In 1971, and again in 1972, Mary became the first woman to win Gold Medals in the Women's World Aerobatic competitions. Mary was unassuming on the terra firma. But, once strapped into her Pitts, Mary Gaffaney became the prima ballerina of the sky winning the U.S. National Women's Aerobatic title five times in a row. Of course, Mary held Air Transport Ratings (now Air Transport Pilot license) in singles, multi-engine and helicopters. She flew fixed-wing, seaplanes, gliders…and probably the boxes they came in! With her husband, she owned Kendall Flying School and Kendall Gliderport near Miami. In 1991, the sky star was inducted into the International Aerobatic Club Hall of Fame. In 2017, at the age of 91, Mary Gaffaney flew West, probably doing loops, rolls, and spins while shouting, "What a wild ride!"

Gardner, Elizabeth L. Remba

"I was called to duty when the war started to learn how to test planes, instruct pilots, tow targets used for anti-aircraft artillery practice, and assemble planes. When I first started learning, I was eager and nervous and also had two days of training under Lieutenant Colonel Paul Tibbetts, who later commanded the B-29 that dropped the first atomic bomb on Hiroshima." WASP Elizabeth Gardner is photographed flying a World War II B-26 Marauder twin-engine, medium bomber. The B-26 was called "the widowmaker" because of the high accident rate. The fast landing speed on final approach could be very intimidating. At slower approach speed, the B-26 would often stall and crash.

(WASP Elizabeth Gardner. U.S. Air Force archive)

Garrow, Maureen

"At age 47, I earned by private certificate and fell in love with aviation. Sharing this passion with students through flight instructing, especially for the 'aha' moments when students achieve understanding. Any day I can fly is a good day, and any day teaching is a great day." In 1995, flight training was her Christmas present, allowing Maureen to fulfill her dream. She continued earning her ratings. By 2015, Maureen became a CFII. In 2016, she became a FAA Gold Seal Flight Instructor. In 2017, and again in 2019, Garrow earned the National Association of Flight Instructors (NAFI) Master Flight Instructor accreditation. The aviation passion Maureen shared before her untimely death reminds us the influence of a good flight instructor can never be erased. Maureen Garrow believed the world of aviation can transform the student forever.

Gervais, Christine

"I have always followed my own path and always felt supported by my family - even if sometimes they questioned some of my 'off the rails' decisions. I never paid much attention to the naysayers. They will be there no matter what you chose for yourself and they didn't know ME. I know ME. That is the singular most important piece of advice I can give you. Know yourself then set your goals and go! – And your goals are allowed to change along the way without anyone else's permission but your own. If you honour yourself, the rest is easy, and sometimes even fun, to deal with. Push YOURself, live outside YOUR comfort zone and grow! It really is that simple." Ms. Gervais serves as the President and CEO of the Canadian Owners and Pilots Association. Christine has aviation industry experience as a commercial pilot and was an air traffic controller in the Ottawa control tower.

Gialloreto, Jaime

"Young girls are our future and we need more of them in STEM and aviation. They are going to be the next generation and role models, so when it comes to aviation, the sky's the limit." Quoted in February2019 *Flight Training* magazine. In 2018, Jaime was Miss New Jersey and a newer student in the field of drones and aviation.

Gillies, Catherine McCann

"My second classman stopped me in the hall because I had just yelled 'Fly Marine Corps, Sir!' He informed me that I couldn't say that since women weren't allowed to fly in the Marine Corps. Ironic, huh?" Quoted June 3, 2014 at www.anneawilson.blogspot.com. As a plebe (freshman) at the U.S. Naval Academy, a requirement was to shout a positive message when encountering an upperclassman. In 1994, Catherine became the U.S. Marine Corps' first woman pilot. The message is clear to be determined and follow your own flight plan.

Gonzalez, Elena

"I was always good with my hands, taking things apart and putting them back together. I used that ability in school for an Airframe & Powerplant (A&P) license and it was a good match." Quoted in July-August 2020 *Aviation for Women* magazine, "Women Who Fix Whatever Flies," by Kathryn B. Creedy. Elena is on the American Airlines aircraft maintenance team. She recently wrote an article about her job and opportunities which appeared in *American Way*, American Airlines In-flight magazine. Elena learned to fly before she could drive. Her message to women thinking about joining this field is to believe you can do it just like our World War II Rosie the Riveters, who blazed the trail 75 years ago.

Greene, Elizabeth "Betty"

"God, I have never heard of anyone who used flying to help spread the Gospel message, but if You want me to fly for You, show me how to make it happen." Reportedly an early prayer of a young Betty Greene, posted at:

https://www.sharihouse.com/post/2016/09/23/hss-betty-greene-navigating-a-storm.

In 1942, private pilot, Betty Greene, joined the WASP. By 1944, assigned to Ohio's Wright Field, she tested high altitude equipment requiring altitudes at 40,000 AGL. In those years, anything above 25,000 AGL was considered extremely dangerous. But, this training would be very valuable later in her aviation career. After the WASP were disbanded, a new door opened. On May 20, 1945 at only age 25, Betty became the co-founder and first mission pilot for Christian Airmen Missionary Fellowship, now known as Mission Aviation Fellowship (MAF). On February 23, 1946, Betty flew the very first mission in a four-seater Waco Cabin Biplane to a Mexican missionary jungle camp which revolutionized the delivery of the Gospel, medical care, food distribution, and more to worldwide remote outposts. Over 30 years, Greene flew MAF flights to Mexico, Peru, Indonesia, Nigeria,

Sudan, Ethiopia, Uganda, Kenya, The Congo, and other countries. Before she retired from active ministry fieldwork, flying a Grumman Duck amphibian, she became one of the few women to fly solo across the Peruvian Andes Mountains. That's where her earlier high altitude flight training was all part of a Divine plan. As she had done in World War II as a WASP, Betty Greene continued to ferry MAF aircraft, as well as provide important MAF leadership at headquarters. Betty flew West in 1997. In 2017, she was selected for the Women in Aviation International Pioneer Hall of Fame.

(Missionary pilot, Betty Greene, on float plane. Courtesy of Mission Aviation Fellowship.)

Hadfield, Robin

"My aviation advice is the same as my non-aviation advice. Think ahead and, even more important, be resilient. Know how to adapt. Always strive to get better." Quoted in July-August 2018, *Ninety-Nines* magazine, "Meet a Governor…Robin Hadfield." A long-time Canadian aviator, Robin shares her experience and leadership through serving as an elected Director on the Board of the International Nine-Nines.

Hamilton, Kelly

"I've spent my adult life being told by people in the system that you can't do that, you're a woman. I have always taken great pleasure in proving them wrong. When it comes to flying, the airplane does not know my gender, it only respects my talent as an aviator." Quoted in *Encyclopedia of Women in Aviation and Space*. In 1970, Kelly was turned down by United Airlines for a flight attendant position "because she looked too much like the girl next door." Her Air Force officer father encouraged her to learn to fly. In 1973, she joined the United States Air Force to do that. Instead, she was one of five women sent to aircraft maintenance. Finally, in 1976 when pilot training opened to women, Hamilton was one of twenty women accepted. She earned her wings to later become only one of five women who were combat-certified to fly the KC-135. During the Gulf War, Kelly Hamilton flew the KC-135. Over her 23-year Air Force career, Colonel Hamilton commanded units, served in public information, and left a legacy that proved women do "Aim High…Fly-Fight-Win!"

Haydu, Bernice "Bee" Falk

"If an engine was overhauled and needed to be flown in a certain manner for a certain number of hours before it went into regular service, I would do that. If personnel had to be flown somewhere in the United States, I flew them wherever they had to go." Quoted in March 9, 2016 *DOD News,* "Fought For Women Vets' Recognition" by Shannon Collins. Haydu had prior aviation training, which was a key factor in her selection to the WASP.

After her training at Avenger Field, WASP Bee Haydu was assigned to Pecos Air Force Base in Texas as an engineering test pilot and general utility pilot for military missions. Bernice earned her nickname, "Bee," because she flew like a Bumble Bee! The WASP were promised that if the "women flying military planes experiment worked out," they would receive military benefits and status. Well, the WASP kept their side of the bargain, but, in 1945 the U.S. Government did not honor its promise to these brave women when the military shut down the WASP program abruptly. The military even classified the WASP files so they remained a "secret" for years. Not until 1977 were WASP finally given the military benefits and recognition they had been promised way back in World War II. Bee Haydu tirelessly led this effort as President of the WASP organization. Haydu, a remarkable leader, aviation business woman, flight instructor, volunteer, and mother is recognized as a member of the Women In Aviation International Pioneer Hall of Fame, winner of the International Ninety-Nines Award of Inspiration, her WASP uniform is on display in the Smithsonian Air and Space Museum, and she is in the New Jersey Aviation Hall of Fame.

Helms, Susan
"I basically decided at a young age - and by young, I mean junior high - that the whole thing of being in the military and particularly the Air Force appealed to me. There were a couple of strong points that I wanted. One of them was the opportunity to travel - little did I know how far that would go - and then also the opportunity for a stable career. I like the idea of moving every few years and seeing different places, and it appeared that my dad had had a very rewarding Air Force career. It looked like, as an engineer, I could also have the same." Quoted from March 1, 2001 NASA Pre-flight interview before Shuttle Discovery Mission STS-102. In 1976, Helms joined the first class of women at the Air Force Academy. As a distinguished graduate of the Air Force Test Pilot School, she has flown over 30 types of Air Force aircraft, including the F-15, F-16, and CF-18 fighters. As a NASA Astronaut, Helms is a five-time space veteran and the first woman to serve on the International

Space Station. Lieutenant General (Ret) Susan Helms was inducted into the Astronauts Hall of Fame. In 2018, she was inducted into the Colorado Women's Hall of Fame.

(Astronaut Susan Helms in space. Courtesy of NASA.)

Hermsdorfer, Jessica

"I could tell it was more serious than anything I'd ever dealt with. I can't recall ever hearing anybody say 'Mayday' before." Quoted in September 2011 *Air & Space,* "Goosed Again" article about her 2010 FAA Archie League Medal of Safety Award for air controllers. As an experienced U.S. Air Force air traffic controller, Hermsdorfer had been trained well for emergency situations. As a 27 year old, she was now a Federal Aviation Administration controller in Kansas City International Airport in the tower providing terminal approach radar. On November 14, 2009 around 7 p.m., Frontier Airlines Flight 820 radioed, "Mayday, mayday. Multiple bird strikes." Now with one engine on fire and the other engine possibly damaged, this airliner with 124 passengers onboard needed to be guided to the runway pronto. Jessica spoke calmly and quickly, clearing out other airlines and guiding the crippled plane's crew to the approach fixes and headings and altitude where it landed safely. But, wait, there is more to this incredible story. After this extremely challenging experience of split second safety decisions, Jessica still had two hours left of her eight-hour shift. And, she had all those other airplanes in the sky waiting to land. So, she kept working! Some background on the "Mayday" call, which is an International distress call signally a life-threatening emergency. Often "Mayday" is said three times in a row so the transmission message is clear. In the 1920s, London's Croydon Airport senior radio officer, Frederick Stanley Mockford, was told to think of an easily communicated word or phrase to be used in emergencies by pilots to airport ground staff. Croydon Airport had high traffic volume from Le Bourget Airport in Paris. "Mayday" was derived from the French phrase "m'aider," which is translated "help me."

Hewson, Marilyn

"The best candidates make a strong case for themselves. They can clearly articulate why they are the best choice for the job-and they can tell me what unique qualities they bring that no one else can offer." Quoted on www.BrainyQuote.com. Since 2015, Hewson was Lockheed

Martin CEO. Recently, she announced her departure from that leadership role. In 1983, she joined the company as an industrial engineer. Since 2010, yearly she has been ranked by *Fortune Magazine* as one of the 50 Most Powerful Women in Business. By 2019, *Forbes* ranked Hewson in the top ten.

Higginbotham, Joan

"After talking to some board members, they suggested I go back and get a more technical advanced degree, which is what I did. It was hard. I'd been back two years earlier. I'd gotten a master's degree. I'd pretty much figured that I was done. And it was hard, too, because I was working full time while getting both of these master's. So I worked essentially night shift so that I could go to the school during the day and get my second degree. But obviously it paid off." Quoted in a NASA story for educators posted December 18, 2006.

https://www.nasa.gov/audience/foreducators/k-4/features/F_MS4_Joan_Higginbotham.html

In 1987, Higginbotham joined NASA at Kennedy Space Center as an engineer. She applied for selection to the Astronaut program. She listened to the advice given to improve her credentials. After earning a second master's degree in space systems, she again applied. In 1996, she became NASA's third female Black American astronaut. In 2006, Higginbotham was part of the seven-member crew on the space shuttle, Discovery.

Howard, Stacy

"If you want to learn about aviation, insurance is an amazing teacher. You gain a whole new perspective when you look at it through the lens of risk management." Quoted August 19, 2018 *State Aviation Journal*, "Stacy Howard Reflects on Her Career in Aviation," by Kim Stevens. As a young widow, aviation provided an opportunity to work in a growing industry immediately. As a private pilot, Stacy was the perfect candidate for the newly-created position with a local insurance brokerage. She quickly learned to provide the service and coverage individual owners, flight training facilities, aircraft repair professionals, airport operators, and commercial air service needed. In 1995, this led Howard to an important role with the Aircraft Owners and Pilots Association (AOPA) as their Regional Representative, working with members and aviation organizations, government and community leaders, sharing the important General Aviation story. Stacy often flew her own airplane. In 2012, the opportunity to serve in a similar role with National Business Aviation Association (NBAA) opened even more opportunity. She continued "living the dream." Now retired, Stacy loves volunteering in the local 99 chapter "Discover Aviation Camp for Girl Scouts." She loves sharing the joy of flight.

Hughes, Christine Angel
"My position as a [certified] Flight Instructor (CFI) is one of my proudest accomplishments in my career. The ability to share the gift of flight with someone is extremely satisfying to me. I will always remember the first time I set foot in a small aircraft for an introductory flight at 16 years old. That feeling is indescribable and I'm excited to help others experience it as well." Quoted September 10, 2020 in *AOPA ePilot,* "Meet Sisters of the Skies Founder, Lt. Christine Angel Hughes," by Jennifer Non. Sisters of the Skies (SOS) is providing a pathway for a new generation of Black female pilots through scholarships, mentoring, and hands-on GRoW-Girls Rock Wings, aviation camps. In 2015, Hughes, currently a U.S. Coast Guard pilot, saw the need and founded SOS. Mentoring and outreach by SOS women in their uniforms impacts young girls who now see Black women in these exciting careers as a new possibility for themselves. Visit: www.SistersoftheSkies.org

Focus more on the people who inspire you than on the ones who annoy you. You'll enjoy life much more and go much further. ~ Unknown

5

J-Juliet to L-Lima

When we discover our power within, we tap into
cosmic vision. ~ Unknown

Jackman, Erika Walker
"When I was learning to fly, a man once asked me why I wanted to be a pilot. He then proceeded to say, 'Women don't fly. If God has intended women to be pilots, He would've made the sky pink and not blue.' I love thinking of all my fellow female aviators when the sunset fills the sky with beautiful pink hues. The sky IS pink!' Quoted in an October 2, 2018 blog on-line at www.princess-awesome.com 'Flying High as a Woman Airline Pilot." That was back in the 1980s, but even today flying as a United States-based major airline pilot, Erika reports that passengers still assume she must be a flight attendant. As a mother of three daughters, Erika wants all girls and the world to know that it's okay to love airplanes, rockets, trucks and trains. It is possible to be anything you want to be, including a princess pilot!

Jackson, Mary W.
"I plan on being an engineer at NASA…I have no choice but to be the first." This was a famous line that was confidently uttered in the court scene in the *Hidden Figures* movie by Janelle Monae, portraying Jackson, fighting for the opportunity to take classes at an all-white school. In 1958, Mary Jackson did become NASA's first African American female engineer. Mary was a gifted math and science student in high school and college. In 1951, after earning duel Bachelor Degrees

in math and physical science at Hampton Institute, Mary secured a research mathematician position at the National Advisory Committee of Aeronautics, which later became NASA. Located in Langley, Virginia, where state law still enforced workplace segregation, separate restrooms had to be used by non-whites. Lunch had to eaten at their desks, instead of in the cafeteria which was "whites-only." But Mary's talent was spotted and mentored. She was encouraged to take engineering classes. By 1978, Mary Jackson became a NASA Human Resource Administrator where she championed women and minorities to advance their careers. In 1985, she retired from NASA. Until her death in 2005, she contributed her time and talent to programs which developed young minds toward math and science. In 2020, NASA renamed its headquarters after Mary W. Jackson to honor her important contributions to our space programs.

Jahn, Gretchen
"I am sort of a novelty-both as a female CEO that is actively flying and racing planes, and as a female CEO of an aircraft equipment manufacturer." Quoted in July 2006, *Airports Journal*, "Mooney CEO Gretchen Jahn: A Welcome Novelty in Aviation," by Airports Journal Staff Writer. Now, as a global advisor to public and private enterprises, Gretchen Jahn is a recognized, dynamic aviation leader. Having transformed Mooney Airplane Company as CEO, the next challenges were General Manager of Alpha Aviation Ltd in New Zealand, then, COO of REMOS Aircraft in Germany. Her list of accomplishments in systems designs, aviation workforce development, and promoting aviation is long. In 1985, she earned her private certificate in a Cessna 150. Over the years, Gretchen owned Cessnas-152, 172, 182, 182RG and 205. Mooney models were added over the years. Hooked on airplanes, she has taken the opportunity to fly Maule, Piper, Beech and a Cirrus. She included DC-3, Mooney Mustang, and L-39 to her growing log book with U.S. commercial pilot certificate, instrument and seaplane ratings, and a New Zealand private pilot license. She is a volunteer and long-time participant in the annual Air Race Classic

(ARC). In 2019, her 30+ years of support to the Ninety-Nines was recognized with their Award of Achievement for Contributions to Aviation.

(Gretchen Air Racer. Courtesy photograph by Donna Crane-Bailey)

James, Deborah Lee

"Always know where you want to go in life, but be prepared to pivot. I wanted to be at the State Department. I wanted to be a diplomat. I didn't get selected. I had to recoup and rebound...I never looked back at the State Department. What originated as a failure early in my life launched me into what became plan B...You learn a lot from failure." Quoted in November 2019, *Military Officer Magazine,* "Set Yourself Up For Success." From 2013 to 2017, James was the 23rd Air Force Secretary, the second woman in our history to hold this leadership position. With over 30 years of management and national security experience, she is the author of *Aim High: Chart Your Course and Find Success.*

Jemison, Mae

"What we find is that if you have a goal that is very, very far out, and you approach it in little steps, you start to get there faster. Your mind opens up the possibilities." Quoted at https://www.inspiringquotes.us. After earning dual degrees at Stanford University in chemical engineering and African-American studies, Jemison earned a Cornell University Doctor of Medicine degree. She applied to the NASA astronaut program and was rejected. In 1988, when she applied again, she was accepted into the program. Dr. Jemison became our first Black female astronaut. In 1992, she completed her Endeavor eight-day mission making her the first Black woman to go into space. Today, Dr. Jemison is a leader in technology and education projects in aerospace.

As corny as it sounds. I love viewing the world from above.~ Leah Mosher, Royal Canadian Air Force Pilot

(Astronaut Mae Jemison. Courtesy of NASA.)

Johnson, Amy

"I think it is a pity to lose the romantic side of flying and simply accept it as a common means of transport, although that end is what we have all ostensibly been striving to attain." Quoted on www.AZquotes.com. One of the first English women to earn a pilot's license. In 1930, she became the first woman to fly solo from Britain to Australia, inspiring many. She died in 1941 as a World War II volunteer pilot in the Women's Auxiliary Air Force when her plane was shot down. In 2016, Johnson was celebrated with induction into the Women in Aviation International Pioneer Hall of Fame.

Johnson, Katherine
"I liked what I was doing, I liked work…My problem was to answer questions, and I did that to the best of my ability at all times." Quoted in September 22, 2017 "Katherine G. Johnson Computational Facility Opens at NASA Langley Research Center," posted at www.goodblacknews.org. Johnson was one of the NASA African American female mathematicians featured in the film, "Hidden Figures." Known as the "human computer" for her skills calculating NASA early space flights in the 1960s.

Jolie, Angelina
"Every time Mad sees a plane, he's amazed. If I could actually fly a plane by the time he's four, I'll be like Superman to him." Quoted in April 19, 2018 *People Magazine*, "Inside Angelina Jolie's Life as a Pilot: From Being Inspired by Maddox to Owning Her Own Plane," by Ale Russian. In 2004, Angelina earned her private pilot rating to the delight of her three-year-old son, Maddox. In 2005, she purchased her Cirrus SR22-G2 with tail number "MX" in his honor. Over the years, she continued her training using this important skill in her work as UN Goodwill Ambassador and Special Envoy to the United Nations High Commissioner for Refugees. Her son, Maddox, is now learning to fly.

Kahn, Karen
"Learn from the mistakes of others. You'll never live long enough to make them yourself! That's the watchword for aviation. As an airline Captain, I read all the accident reports trying to absorb the pertinent details for use in flight and on the ground. I recall an eye-opening incident during my career when my clumsiness caused some real havoc…when I fumbled my water bottle and squirted liquid over a panel that controls our electronic map display…Upon landing I called our

maintenance techs and 'fessed up,' describing my faux pas and the type of liquid involved. It turns out that water was okay, as a hair dryer would dry it, and the instruments would recover. Soda or coffee, on the other hand, was not okay, as those would leave a residue which mandated the equipment be replaced…Mess up? Fess up…Hiding mistakes can be deadly…mistakes can be your best friends, if you'll learn quickly from them and use the knowledge wisely in the future." Quoted from July 7, 2014 blog http://captainkarenkahn.blogspot.com/ web site www.CaptainKarenKahn.com. Kahn is a Charter Member of the International Society of Women Airline Pilots-ISA+21.

Kalishek, Karen Ann
"There's always more to learn and tantalizing aviation adventures await. I have a bucket list of new experiences yet to explore and have enjoyed aerial treats such as wing-walking on a Stearman's top wing during loops, rolls and hammerhead maneuvers." Quoted from April 16, 2019 *Civil Air Patrol News*, "Wis. Wing Pilot Honored as National FAA Safety Team Representative of the Year," by Sheila Pursglove. Kalishek was a "late bloomer." Her first flight lesson was at age 33 but she delayed pursuing aviation until age 50 when she earned her private pilot certificate. Since then she focused her talent, skill, and years as an educator into a ten-year plan. She is a National Association of Flight Instructors' Master Flight Instructor-twice and volunteers as a NAFI Board member. She is a FAA Gold Seal Instructor, a Cirrus Training Center Instructor, and provides private flight instruction. She is an active member of her Experimental Aircraft Association chapter, Ninety-Nines, and Women in Aviation International member. She serves as a Civil Air Patrol safety officer, public affairs officer, check pilot, and assistant aerospace education officer, all as a volunteer. Karen Ann Kalishek is living proof of what Oprah Winfrey described as "Passion is energy. Feel the power that comes from focusing on what excites you."

Kardon, Robin "R.D."

"My goal was to realistically recreate the discriminatory environment, harassment, and challenges I faced as a female pilot. It is only through an examination of our past that we can help shape a better future both on the ground and in the air." Quoted in January 10, 2019 *General Aviation News*, "The not so friendly skies." Robin is a San Diego pilot. She based her debut novel, FLYGIRL, on her 12 years of corporate aviation experience. As a rated pilot, Kardon entered an all-male corporate flight department in the 1990s.

Kaufmann, Lara

"When people think about a career in aviation, a commercial airline pilot, who has to spend a lot of time away from home, often comes to mind. Many times those who want to start a family choose careers in other industries without ever researching all the different employment opportunities available in aviation. If you love aircraft, I encourage you to consider all your options in this great field. Your dream job awaits!" Lara Kaufmann is the Associate Director of the Greenville Downtown Airport in South Carolina, the first woman to serve on the South Carolina Aeronautics Commission, Co-Chair of the National Air Transportation Association's General Aviation Airports Committee, and sits on the Greenville Tech Aircraft Maintenance Technology Advisory Committee.

Kelley, Erin

"I love seeing female performers and pilots, but I want young women to know there is room in the maintenance field also." Quoted in the March/April 2019 WAI *Aviation For Women*, "Crew Chief Erin Kelley: Caretaker of a MiG," by Kelly Nelson. Erin began her aviation journey in the U.S. Navy, starting as a ground handler, parking, and fueling a variety of military aircraft. Then, she tackled avionics training. Next was the maintenance team for the F/A-18s. After 14 years of active duty, Kelley returned home to Texas where a chance visit to the Tyler Historic Aviation Memorial Museum at the Tyler Pounds Regional Airport led to meeting the president of Fighter Jets Inc. where, over time, Erin demonstrated such obvious high standards and competence, she was asked to be their air show crew chief. Now, most air show weekends fans will see the lone woman crew chief on the line decked out in her signature pink headsets, t-shirt, shoe laces and even pink wands for night shows. Erin greets air show fans with the enthusiasm she feels for aviation.

Keown-Blackburn, Janis

"As a child I was thrilled by airplanes and stopped to look every time I saw one. I would wonder who was in the plane and where they were going. I wanted to be up there." In 1968, stewardess for Eastern Airlines became her career goal. But, they turned her down. She moved to a flying career as a private flight instructor and continued to earn advanced ratings, even flying charters. Then, in 1980, Janis became the very first female pilot of Princeton Airways. By 1984, she became the first and only female pilot at Sun Country Airlines. Just five months later, Eastern Airlines offered her an opportunity as a second officer. Her dream had come full circle, except now she was in the front of that passenger plane. She became the first female Airbus A 300 crew member in the United States. Sharing her love for aviation in a children's book, *Teddy, The Airplane*, Janis hopes to inspire a whole generation of new aviators.

Kern, Rose Marie

"As a young divorced mother I needed to have a good, solid career in order to raise my daughters in a safe and comfortable environment. I learned to stand my ground when others tried to trip me up and over time I became one of the best at my job." After a 34-year career in the Federal Aviation Administration (FAA) Air Traffic Control System, Rose Marie shares insights into this fascinating aviation career in her book, *Stress is Relative: Memoir of An Air Traffic Controller.*

Kimbrell, Shawna Rochelle

"It's really hard to build a road, if you don't know where you're going. A lot of people have goals, but don't really put them into context. If a goal is really your end state, you have to look at the terrain you have to go through to get there, how you're going to build that road and what you're going to do. Nothing's easy. Expect road blocks, expect that there are going to be people out there who don't want you to succeed, expect people are going to tell you no. But the desire that comes from within -- if it's something that you really want -- will carry you through." Quoted from February 23, 2012, *U.S. Air Force News.* In 1998, Kimbrell graduated for the U.S. Air Force Academy. In 1999, Shawna earned her pilot wings. She became the U.S. Air Force's first Black female fighter pilot. In 2001, she flew her first combat mission in Iraq in Operation Northern Watch. She flew the multi-million dollar F-16.

(Fighter Pilot Kimbrell. U.S. Air Force photo by Airman 1ˢᵗ class Ashley Wood)

King, Debbie Travis

"I can't say it is easy. These are the things you're going to have to buckle up for…and we can do it." Quoted July 21, 2014 *USA TODAY* Network-Wisconsin, "Meet B-29 pilot Debbie Travis King," by Noell Dickmann. Travis is the only woman in the world since the World War II WASP authorized to fly the iconic Boeing B-29 Superfortress. She pilots "FIFI" of the Commemorative Air Force, the only airworthy B-29 left. King grew up with airplanes both flying and "fixing." them. She began earning her flight certificates and ratings in high school and continued through college. She earned CFI/CFII quickly after college graduation, followed by jet ratings and the Air Transport Pilot certificate. She flew corporate jets as a charter pilot. Debbie pilots the CAF B-24 Liberator and others in their CAF fleet of historical significance. All these years after the WASP demonstrated that women can fly military bombers, Debbie Travis King still experiences disbelief that a woman can "fly that thing." Debbie is now the CAF WASP Squadron Leader which serves as an historic reminder that over 75 years ago women already "have been there and done that." The opportunity is just as rewarding today for women to take flight.

Koch, Christina

"We always had *National Geographic* and *Astronomy* magazines, and *Popular Mechanics* lying around the house. I got interested in exploration and different parts of the world and different parts of the Universe just from seeing those things around the house…" Quoted on www.Brainyquote.com. In 2013, Koch was selected for NASA space exploration. Her areas of expertise are space science instrument development and remote scientific field engineering. She is a Polar explorer and record-setting NASA astronaut on the International Space Station. Koch performed six spacewalks. The first three were conducted by an all-female team. She holds the record for the longest single flight by a woman, 328 days in space.

(NASA Christina Koch EMU. Courtesy of NASA.)

Kukla, Sandra
"I figured out I know a lot more about aviation than the average architect, and it's really a great building type. I decided from that point that I really wanted to do aviation architecture." Quoted May 28, 2020 *State Aviation Journal Focus*. As the new President of DWL Architects in Phoenix and a licensed pilot, Sandra combines her personal interest and understanding of airports, operations, and the important passenger

experience into her architectural designs for airports. Projects range from new expansions to redesign of existing airport facilities across the Southwest.

Lascomb, Jordan
"The best advice that I can give someone who is motivated to pursue this career is to take everything one step at a time. When you look at the big picture of all of the steps you will accomplish to become an airline pilot, it can be daunting. If you focus on what is in front of you, one check ride at a time, one flight at a time, you will eventually be looking back on a career of accomplishments and be amazed at where you stand! This career is worth every moment of stress along the way." Quoted April 2, 2018, *Flying's Airline Pilot News*, "Professional Pilot Profile: Jordon Lascomb," by *Flying* staff. Initially drawn to airplanes by jumping out of them as a skydiver, Jordon felt comfortable in the air. For her 21st birthday, a tandem skydive started her love affair with the sky. After more than 200 jumps, Lascomb began her adventure in the cockpit with flight lessons. Now, as a first officer with a regional airline and one of their pilot recruiters, she still loves the sky and the views are always changing out her flying office window!

Latimer, Mary
"I take more pride and joy in the achievements that I have helped others leverage and by building a foundation for female fliers." Quoted in March-April 2018 *Ninety-Nines* magazine, "Mary Latimer: Flying and Inspiring," by Sue Mead. In 2011, in a "someone should do that…that somebody will be me" moment while visiting the wonderful WASP WWII Museum in Sweetwater, TX. Mary realized that all-woman training environment was successful back then so she founded GIFT-Girls in Flight Training. This legacy builder knows how important having mentors and support are. In 1973, at age 19, she enrolled in the local A & P training program. She was the only female in the class of 125. She even bought her own airplane, an Aeronca L-3 to shorten her commute and build hours and experience. In a year, Mary earned her

aircraft mechanic certificate, along with commercial and flight instructor ratings. Because of gender, many doors where slammed shut on her. Then, encouragement came from the FAA for her to apply for air traffic control. In 1976, she began that flight path. Once again Mary was the only female in her class. In 1977, she earned Inspection Authorization when the FAA legal counsel intervened and "ordered" the local FSDO (Flight Service District Office) to administer the test. In 2002, Mary Latimer retired from ATC. But, her love of aviation continued through flight instruction and now GIFT.

Leavitt, Jeannie
"I truly see diversity as a competitive advantage. What we really want to get at is that diversity of thought. If I have people around the table who think differently, who have different backgrounds, then we're going to come to a better solution–it's going to take longer; there will be vastly different opinions, but we're going to get to a better solution in the end." Quoted from her 2018 TED "Women Spotlight" talk. U.S. Air Force Major General Leavitt has 3,000 flight hours, including more than 300 in combat over Iraq and Afghanistan. In 2020, she was inducted into Women in Aviation International Pioneer Hall of Fame.

Lefkowitz, JaNette
"Don't worry so much about what other people say or whatever other people think. Just keep doing what you're doing. Just keep doing the right things, and just keep going, and don't worry about the setbacks. And enjoy." Quoted in February 2020 *Parachutist* magazine, "Chasing Gold-JaNette Lefkowitz Tells the Whole Epic Tale," by Annette O'Neill. In 2001, JaNette's uncle first introduced this champion jumper with a tandem jump. This gal was hooked. She completed her MIT Mechanical Engineering degree, but, her heart was in the sky. She has more than 10,000 skydives and hundreds of Wind Tunnel Time hours. In 2007, she co-founded SDC-Rhythm XP with her husband. This successful sky diving school and also award-winning professional team are internationally known. In 2019 at the U.S. Parachute Association

Nationals, they earned gold. In 2016, Lefkowitz won gold at the World Parachuting Championships as a member of our U.S. Women's Team, the Army Golden Knights. She shares her passion for the sport through the Women's Skydiving Network (WSN). She is one of the founding members. WSN enables and encourages up-and-coming women skydivers to reach their skydiving goals. WSN connects them with prominent women leaders in the sport. Skills to improve teaching in the tunnel and in the sky are part of WSN mission. Other ways WSN assists women jumpers is with instructor and coach ratings, perfecting their canopy skills, and work toward state, national, and even a world record jumps. JaNette and her joy remind me of the quote, "Find out what gives you joy and do it!"

Lindbergh, Anne Morrow
"It takes as much courage to have tried and failed as it does to have tried and succeeded." Quote from www.BrainyQuote.com. In 1930, Anne was the first woman to earn a U.S. glider pilot's license. In 1932, she helped her husband, Charles, pioneer Airline Industry routes. In order to do so, she learned Morse code and earned a radio operator's license. Celebrated writer of many important works, including *North to the Orient, Listen to the Wind*, and *Gift from the Sea*. In 1979, she was selected for the National Aviation Hall of Fame. In 1982, she was selected for the Katharine Wright Award. In 1999, she was honored by inclusion in the Women Aviation International Pioneer Hall of Fame. In 2001, Anne Morrow Lindbergh died quietly in her Vermont home.

Lindheim, Mindy
"When pilots can connect online, it creates a new motivation to do what you love knowing that you have like-minded people to share your experience with." Quoted from September 2020, *EAA Sport Aviation Magazine*, "Good Influence" by Beth E. Stanton. Mindy is a strong advocate for promoting aviation on social media. As Regional Sales Director for Textron Aviation, she has a large Instagram, YouTube, and aviation podcasts community where she shares the exciting benefits of

aviation and her aircraft sales position. Mindy flies almost daily demonstrating Cessna and Beechcraft planes. In addition to assisting aviation mechanics, Mindy earned her ratings using aviation scholarships, trading work for instruction, and even worked as a flight school scheduler to reduce costs. She earned instrument, commercial, and CFI and II, and now is a Textron Demo pilot team member. To Mindy flying, freedom, and flexibility are the benefits which need to be shared widely with a new generation of aviators and airplane owners.

London, Barbara Jane "BJ" Erickson
"I think it was a tremendous opportunity that I was given and I'm thankful for it." Quoted on WASP Final Flight at https://waspfinalflight.blogspot.com/2013/07/barbara-jane-bj-erickson-london-wafs.html. Barbara was the only woman awarded an Air Medal in World War II for successfully completing an 8,000-mile air mission. Barbara was the youngest member of the Women's Auxiliary Ferry Squadron (WAFS) and one of their original 25 members. During the time she was a WASP, she flew almost every make and model of military aircraft. In 1940, while still in college, she worked as a "Rosie the Riveter" at the Boeing B-17 factory. Barbara Erickson, applied and was accepted into the Civilian Pilot Training Program. She earned land and seaplanes ratings. She became a flight instructor. In October, 1942, she completed her first air mission of World War II. She became one of the few women who built, and later flew the Flying Fortress B-17 bomber. During the War Years, she led a flight squadron of up to 60 women pilots in Long Beach, CA. They flew factory airplanes for delivery to our military bases. After the WASP were disbanded, she married another pilot. She received a commission as a Major in the reserves. She served in that capacity for 20 years. Barbara applied to the airlines to continue as a commercial pilot. They all turned her down and several sent her applications for stewardess instead. Undaunted, she successfully sold aircraft. For more than 30 years, "BJ" helped run the All Women's Transcontinental Air Race (AWTAR). In 2005, London

became a member of our Women in Aviation International Pioneer Hall of Fame.

Luebke, Patricia

"Two of my favorite guiding principles, which work for worry and for other situations as well. Part one is, 'Take a positive action.' ...Just do something. Part two is, 'The universe rewards action.' ...Try it." Pat wrote this in one of her last "Personal Development" columns in May/June 2019 WAI *Aviation for Women* magazine. Pat was a gifted and insightful writer for several aviation publications throughout her career to include *Avionics News*, Sporty's, Aircraft Owners and Pilots Association *Pilot* magazine, and Lightspeed Aviation.

(Senior Airman Eunbi Ko serves in Aerospace Medicine. Air National Guard photograph by Staff Sgt. Jacob Cessna)

6
M-Mike to N-November

The difference between a stumbling block and a stepping
stone, is how we view them. ~ Anonymous

Mann, Nicole Aunapu
"I'm probably one of the few astronauts who *didn't* know that's what I wanted to do as a kid. 'Astronaut' seemed like a far-fetched dream. I'm from Penngrove, California, and it wasn't until my first tour in Iraq flying fighter jets with the Marine Corps that I realized one day I might actually be a good candidate. Going into space will be the absolute coolest thing in the world." Quoted on January 7, 2016 on www.rocket-women.com regarding a recent *Glamour Magazine* feature, "Fearless NASA Astronauts." In 1999, Nicole graduated from the U.S. Naval Academy as a Marine Corps officer. In 2003, she earned her Naval Aviator Wings of Gold. She was deployed twice on aircraft carriers in support of Iraq and Afghanistan combat operations. Later, Mann was a test pilot in the F/A-18 Hornet and Super Hornet. In June 2013, she was selected as a NASA astronaut.

Markham, Linda
"You have to have a passion for what you do. I would say anyone who has a passion for what they do will succeed." Quoted in May-June 2015, WAI *Aviation For Women* magazine, "Up from HR: Linda Markham at the helm of Cape Air," by Kathryn B. Creedy. Upon her arrival at Cape Air, the airline served 17 cities and employed about 300. Now, Cape Air

reaches 44 cities in six regions around the world and has more than 1,200 employees. Cape Air Human Resources Department grew with new responsibilities to support that success. Linda is a Holyoke Community College graduate with a degree in business and retail management. Over her career she learned the value of team work and building team members. In addition to leading Cape Air, Linda Markham is a busy mother, community volunteer and the WAI Board Chair.

Mazzu, Tristan
"My greatest hope is that this commercial can be encouragement for women to push through adversity in the work-place, and to show the next generation of female pilots that if flying is something you want to do, you can do it." May/June 2019 WAI *Aviation for Women*, "The Beauty That Breeds Confidence," by Tristan in her own words. She shares the backstory of the filming of the popular Olay commercials, "A Love Letter to Adversity" featuring Tristan in her role as airline pilot. The tag line, "There is nothing more beautiful than a woman on a mission," is at the end of these inspiring commercials. https://vimeo.com/280580712 (Olay Pilot Life) https://vimeo.com/280578311 (Olay "Gratitude")

McAuliffe, Christa
"I touch the future. I teach." Quoted from www.BrainyQuote.com On January 28, 1986, our first "Teacher in Space," Christa, and her NASA space shuttle orbiter crew members were all tragically killed in a massive explosion, only seventy-three seconds into their Challenger launch. Christa McAuliffe was the first civilian NASA selected to bring science and space directly in to the classroom.

It is not the things we did we might regret but the things we didn't do. ~ Unknown

(Astronaut Crista McAuliffe. NASA photograph.)

McCart, Jean Francis

"...being a WASP impacted my life in many ways...[It] gave me a lot of confidence in myself and provided me with wonderful, lifelong friends." Quoted on www.waspfinalflight.blogspot.com/2011. Jean was a World War II Women's Airforce Service Pilot. WASP flew 60,000,000 miles in every type of U.S. Army aircraft with many missions. In the post-War era, Jean was an Aerobatic Flight Instructor. The Library of Congress Stories from the Veterans History Project has several interviews with former WASP at:

https://www.loc.gov/vets/stories/ex-war-wasp.html.

McClain, Anne

"The biggest thing is not to give up. If you stay focused on that goal, you can shape your life in that direction." Quoted in February 17, 2019 NPR Weekend Edition with Lulu Garcia-Navario www.npr.org/2019/02/17/695536882/every-day-is-a-good-day-when-you-re-floating-anne-mcclain-talks-life-in-space. U.S. Military Academy graduate and engineer with more than 2,000 flight hours in 20 different aircraft, she was selected to join the NASA Astronaut program as a Flight Engineer on the International Space Station. She has 203 days in space with two space walks.

McIver, Ivy

"My advice is don't apologize, don't fit into a niche, and follow a certain path. Just go do it and follow your passion." Quoted in July/August 2019, WAI *Women For Aviation* magazine, "The GA Lifestyle: Connecting Owners with the Freedom of Flight," by Kelly Murphy. McIver, Amy Voss, Sarah Talucci, and Beth Duff are teamed at Cirrus Aircraft in training, sales, and customer service. Although each took their own paths to Cirrus, they feel their success can help change the face of the industry and demonstrate how successful a company can be in an inclusive and supportive environment.

McKeown, Heather

"Life's tough. Life is so full of the negative...but, if you hang on, you just may learn from whatever it is you're going through right now." Quoted from her *Optimist* newspaper. Heather McKeown, author of *Above and Beyond: Inspiring Adventures Into The Blue,* eventually had a career as a Flight Attendant. Originally rejected 53 times by Canadian airlines between ages 18 to 22. She temporarily put her airline dream on hold. Finally, many years later, an airline did not think "she was too short!" Heather proved it is never too late to make your dreams come true.

McNevin, Heather

"My advice for mentoring is simple. Find someone who geeks out at the same stuff you do and develop that bond. Also, having an airport dog never hurts." Heather wrote in the May-June 2015 WAI *Aviation For Women* magazine, "Unintentional Mentors," about her aviation journey. In 1996, at the ripe age of 14, she started flight lessons at the local FBO with a young-at-heart World War II veteran pilot. Then, the local FBO was sold to a couple who quickly accepted the young airport kid, especially "Jake," who allowed Heather to follow her on her airport duties, along with Jake's dog. Jake helped Heather study for her private pilot license and taught her all about the FBO business. Everything, not just how to fuel airplanes. How to file NOTAMS, talk "aviation" on the UNICOM, change windsocks and runway lights. Mastering mowing and snow-plowing were included in the many life lessons of a good airport FBO. "Dawg" even adopted Heather who took him flying with her. Over the years, Heather earned advanced certificates and ratings-CFI, CFII, and MEI. She also became an air traffic controller. With every success, she gladly shares the credit with her FBO mentors. Research released in May 2020 found mentored women are statistically much more successful in the workplace. Also, they rise more quickly to higher positions and leadership in their industry.

McSally, Martha

"Before I became a fighter pilot, everyone said that women didn't have the physical strength. Well, I had just completed the Hawaii Ironman Triathlon." Quoted on www.inspiringquotes.us. McSally was America's first woman to fly a fighter jet in combat and the first woman in U.S. history to command a fighter squadron, also in combat. She deployed six times to the Middle East and Afghanistan, flying 325 combat hours in the A-10 "Warthog," earning a Bronze Star and six Air Medals. After a 26-year military career, retiring at the rank of Colonel, she later was elected to the U.S. House of Representatives. She is currently serving in the U.S. Senate representing Arizona.

Medaris-Culea, Patti

"Oooh! What are all those pretty little lights?" Quote from *One-way or Round Trip: Women Flight Attendants and Troops during the Vietnam War*. On that October, 1967, dawn approach of the Flying Tiger Line Boeing 707 into DaNang Airport, South Vietnam, the pilot matter-of-factly responded, "They're shooting at us." The new flight attendant in this war zone quickly learned the lights were tracers followed by bullets. Patti's dream was to become a combat, jet fighter pilot. In 1962, that was out of reach for Patti and other women. To be in the air, she became a Bonanza Airlines stewardess. She seized the opportunity to join our military in Vietnam as a civilian, Flying Tiger Line stewardess. From 1966 to 1975, more than 1,000 brave flight attendants helped airlift many of the 2,700,000 American men and women, who served in the Vietnam War. Nearly all of those flight attendants were women just like Patti. Their stories need to be recorded in the history of women who served our nation during the Vietnam War.

Mendieta, Arlene

"Amelia Earhart is a powerful inspiration for all of us – not only for her accomplishments in aviation, but also for her role in challenging popular notions of a woman's place in society. I'm thrilled to be tracing Amelia's flight across America and along the way, sharing the story of a remarkable woman who deserves to be remembered for her life, not just her disappearance." Quote in August 25, 2019 *Minot Daily News*. In September, 2001, California Ninety-Nine, Dr. Mendieta, recreated Amelia Earhart's 1928 record-setting cross-country-New York to California and back flight. Flying a 1927 Avro Avian, similar to Amelia's. Arlene landed in 23 cities, sharing her love of aviation.

Metcalf-Lindenburger, Dorothy Marie "Dottie"

"So, why did I want to work for NASA? I wanted to be part of exploration. I didn't want to watch from the outside-to only glean information from the planetarium, books, and my science teacher. I wanted to be on the 'inside,' living the excitement of exploring our solar system on a daily basis." Quoted from *Colorado's Astronauts: In their Own Words*. In 2004, Dottie was selected as a Mission Specialist. She served on the STS-131 crew and logged 362 hours in space. In 2014, she retired from NASA.

Mintzmyer, Angela

"A career in aviation doesn't just mean 'pilot.' It is a multi-dimensional, continually expanding industry. No matter what your background is, if you have a passion for aviation, now is the time to pursue your career goals." Quoted July 2, 2020 in *Flagstaff Business News*, "Advocating for Women in Aviation," by Sue Marceau. Angela is the general manager of North-Aire Aviation flight training school at Prescott Regional Airport. Imagine "herding cats" and you will understand the fast-paced, multi-tasking skills needed. Scheduling aircraft, flight instructors, students, staff, managing expenses, keeping maintenance logs, high-touch and high-tech customer service. High energy and flexibility are important traits to meet the daily challenges in this important airport business.

Morgan, JoAnn

"All of my mentors were men. That's just a plain fact and that needs to be acknowledged. …You have to realize that everywhere I went — if I went to a procedure review, if I went to a post-test critique, almost every single part of my daily work — I'd be the only woman in the room. I had a sense of loneliness in a way, but on the other side of that coin, I wanted to do the best job I could…I look at that picture of the firing room where I'm the only woman (Apollo 11). And I hope all the pictures now that show people working on the missions to the Moon and onto Mars, in rooms like Mission Control or Launch Control or wherever — that there will always be several women. I hope that photos like the one I'm in don't exist anymore." Quoted in NASA July 12, 2019 interview, "Rocket Fuel in Her Blood: The Story of JoAnn Morgan." In 1963, she became the first female engineer at NASA Kennedy Space Center (KSC). She was the first woman division chief, the first woman senior executive, the first woman KSC associate director, and the first woman director of Safety and Mission Assurance. Her NASA engineering career spanned 40 years.

Murphy, Sally Dale
"I was the only woman in Army Aviation School in the early 70s and if I told you I did not have problems with a few people, I would not be truthful. But things were changing and with the Vietnam War winding down, the Army needed to fill some voids. There were some tough times but it made me stronger. The Army is a family and there was always someone giving me encouragement and ready to assist me anytime I needed help." Quoted April 2, 2009 in Aero Network. In 1974, at age 25, Sally became the Army's first woman helicopter pilot with her graduation at Fort Rucker. Over her Army career, she served in several staff and leadership roles. In 1999, Colonel Murphy retired.

Nelson, Remoshay "Mesha"
"I now understand that life is truly like flying an airplane. You will experience weather delays, bird strikes, and turbulences on your journey. These are all things you cannot control. The only thing you can do is focus on how you react to these things. Life is about 10% what happens to us and 90% of how we react to it. Therefore, always try to focus your energy on the things you can change, being positive and confident." Quoted in *2020 WAI Aviation for Girls*, "Precision Performance," by Captain Remoshay Nelson. As an Air Force Public Affairs Officer and now a pilot in her first season with the Thunderbirds Air Demonstration Squadron, her greatest challenge was believing in her own abilities. Taking on new roles and opportunities for advancement were important. As a child, role models as Bessie Coleman, Astronaut Mae Jemison, Olympian Wilma Rudolph, and others helped show her other Black women had achieved greatness. Soon, she tried to imitate their hard work, drive, and overcame challenges.

Nelson, Sara

"They gave their lives to the union, and made it possible for other women to have this career and be mothers and have our benefits." Quoted in the February 11, 2020, *Fortune The Broadsheet* "Parting Words" by Claire Zillman. Sara is the president of the world's largest Flight Attendant union, Association of Flight Attendants CWA. She respects the many personal sacrifices women made who preceded her. As early as May 15, 1930, Ellen Church, a pilot, wanted to fly in that position. Because of her gender, that airline door was slammed shut. She was also a registered nurse so she convinced Boeing Air Transport, United's predecessor, to hire her as an "air hostess." What better way to calm passengers and provide caring service? After all, if a woman was working in the aircraft, it must be safe! Other airlines followed suit and "Sky Girls" were soon providing passenger services. In the 1940s, a union formed, known as the Airline Stewardess Association (ALSA). By the 1950s, the positions were portrayed as glamorous and exciting. Strict weight, height, and age requirements were the norm for hiring. Some airlines even grounded women older than age 32. In 1957, TWA dropped the requirement that flight attendants had to be single. Most women were fired or had to quit if they married. In 1956, the first Miss Skyway beauty pageant was held. Braniff "air hostess," Muffett Webb, was crowned the winner. In 1964, with the passage of the Civil Rights legislation and formation of an Equal Opportunity Commission with formal channels to file gender and age discrimination complaints. Airline allowed males to be married or continue to fly beyond age 35 needed to change. In 1966, Mary Sproges resigned her position because of marriage. She filed an EEO complaint for sex discrimination against the airline. In 1968, United Airlines agreed upon a settlement that women on the payroll could keep their jobs. However, it took another three years, for flight attendant positions to actually open up to married women. In the 1970s, the more gender-neutral "Flight Attendant" began to be used. Finally on July 10, 1986, a long fought law suit seeking back pay and re-instatement for 475 former flight attendants forced to quit their position in the 1960s because of the no-marriage rule, were awarded back pay and allowed to fly again.

Nichols, Ruth

(Ruth Nichols. Library of Congress archive)

"It takes special kinds of pilots to break frontiers, and in spite of the loss of everything, you can't clip the wings of their hearts." Quoted on the National Aviation Hall of Fame web site about the accomplishments of this remarkable aviator, inducted into that Hall of Fame in 1992. In 1929, Ruth Rowland Nichols was a charter member of The Ninety-Nines, International Organization of Women Pilots. Nichols is the only woman to hold simultaneous world records for speed, altitude, and distance. She was the first woman in the world to obtain a hydroplane license. During her lifetime (1901-1960), she flew every type of aircraft developed-dirigible, glider, auto gyro, seaplanes, biplanes, triplanes, transport aircraft, and a supersonic jet. In 1958, at age 57, as co-pilot, she set new women's world records for altitude (51,000 feet) and speed (1,000 miles per hour) in a TF-102A Delta Dagger.

Noyes, Blanche Wilcox
"In the air I feel above all petty things, it's like a religion with me." Quoted October 19, 1981, *The Washington Post*, "Blanche Noyes Was Pioneer in U.S. Aviation." Born in 1900 in Cleveland, the same year the Ohio Wright Brothers began their first manned glider experiments, destiny would propel Blanche to future aviation fame. Smart and attractive, she left a promising movie and theater career to marry airmail pilot, Dewey Noyes. In 1929, he bought her an airplane and taught her to fly. A natural aviator, she quickly became the first licensed female pilot in Ohio. That same year, she also entered the Women's Air Derby from Santa Monica to Cleveland, placing fourth, right behind the famous Amelia Earhart. Noyes was a charter member of the Ninety-Nines. In the early 1930s, Blanche flew as a demonstration pilot for Standard Oil and other corporations during those lean years of the Great Depression. In 1935, Dewey was killed in an airplane crash. Now, a widow, Noyes became passionate about pilot and aviation safety. In 1936, she joined the Bureau of Air Commerce Air Marking Group of the Bureau of Air Commerce (forerunner of the FAA). That same year, Blanche joined Louise Thaden to shatter stereotypes to win the coveted Bendix National Transcontinental Air Race. They flew a Beechcraft C17R Staggerwing, powered by a Wright whirlwind nine-cylinder radial engine. For over 35 years, Noyes worked tirelessly to formalize our National air marking program. For many years, she was the only

woman pilot allowed to fly a federal government airplane. Noyes taught aviation safety and published many articles about the topic. In 1970, she was inducted into the National Aviation Hall of Fame. Also, Blanche Noyes became the first woman to receive a gold medal from the Commerce Department for her years of dedication to aviation safety.

(Blanche Noyes. Library of Congress archive)

Nutter, Zoe Dell Lantis

"Get out there with what you've got, because you never know how you'll get to use it." Quoted in *Profiles of Ohio Women 1903-2003* by Jacqueline Jones Royster. What a full life this "First Lady of Aviation" lived. Encouraged early for public performances, especially dance, Zoe traded hard work--washing clothes and dishes, for dance lessons while still a teenager. After high school, this intrepid gal took her life savings and traveled alone to San Francisco to perform in the ballet. In 1939, after several outstanding performances, the Golden Gate International

Exposition being held on the famed Treasure Island hired Zoe to nationally promote aviation and their event. Dressed in a "pirate costume," Zoe flew over 100,000 passenger miles to meet governors and mayors across the United States, speaking on the safety and comforts of air travel. Life magazine declared Zoe pictured on their front cover, "the most photographed woman in the world." Soon, Paramount Pictures signed her for a short film career. During World War II, she joined the USO to entertain the troops. Settling in northern California, she soon became a private pilot for the convenience flying offered. In 1958, Standard Oil of California asked Zoe to represent them in Brussels, Belgium at the World's Fair. She continued to effectively promote commercial air travel around the world. In the early 1960s, Piper Aircraft made her their spokesperson for General Aviation, just as she had done for years for commercial aviation. She demonstrated aircraft and promoted flight training and safety. In 1965, Zoe married Ervin Nutter, the owner of Elano Corporation which produced tubing and engine components for the aerospace industry. Her flying expertise and marketing prowess, complemented her husband's extensive technical expertise. Soon Zoe was one the Elano Corporation pilots and directed projects in the small aircraft division. Zoe worked on the development of a better manifold for more air power. Later, her design became accepted standard equipment which reduced engine maintenance and allowed for a quieter, better-heated cabin. Zoe logged 2,000 flight hours, earned commercial, instrument, and multi-engine ratings. She served as a search and rescue pilot for the Ohio Civil Air Patrol. She was the first woman President of the National Aviation Hall of Fame. In 2008, she was inducted into the Living Legends of Aviation.

Nyberg, Karen
"I love to create. I would really like people to see you can have a job like this, which is very technical, and still have hobbies that are not." Quoted March 18, 2013 NASA "The Softer Side of Space: A Profile of Astronaut Karen Nyberg." As our 50th woman to launch into space, Nyberg grew up in Minnesota. In 1994, she earned a mechanical

engineering degree, Summa Cum Laude, from the University of North Dakota. She interned at NASA and worked in astronaut support until joining the NASA Astronaut Corps. Along the way she earned advanced degrees and gained insight into NASA systems. In 2008, Karen flew as Discovery STS-124 crew. In 2013, she returned to space spending six months on the International Space Station as Flight Engineer on Expedition 36/37. In 2020, after 30 years at NASA, Dr. Nyberg retired.

(NASA astronaut Karen Nyberg in space cupola. NASA photograph)

Touch the Sky. Be in harmony with the clouds and the wind. ~ Unknown

7
O-Oscar to R-Romeo

I will create a new sky trail for others to follow.
~ Unknown

O'Neill, Nora
"While working as a 23-year old flight instructor in Alaska, 'the boys,' I call them boys because they were immature, told the company owner, 'We don't want to work for a company with a woman. It is embarrassing to us.' I felt horrible and wanted to quit. But, if I quit, they would win." Quoted in YouTube interview December 18, 2013 titled "Flying Tigress: She Lifts Off series." Nora was the first woman pilot for Alaska Central Air (1974), and also The Flying Tiger Line (1976). She was the first woman in the world to pilot the Douglass DC-8 (1977), and first to fly passengers in a Boeing 747 (1980). She was the first woman airline pilot to land in Korea, Japan, The Philippines, Malaysia, Saudi Arabia, and Hong Kong. A founding member of ISA+21. She retired from Federal Express with 35 years and 22,000 hours.

Pandit, Aarohi
"This project was so much more than just a circumnavigation; it was about representing women in aviation and marking India on the world map of aviation. Since gratitude is the only attitude, I will always be thankful to my instructors, my mentors, and all the people around the world who helped me in every step." Quoted in July-August 2020,

Ninety-Nines magazine, "Aarohi Pandit Around the World in a Light Sport Aircraft," by Jann Clark, Eastern New England Chapter. Inspired at age seven at the airport by just seeing a striking female airline pilot, Aarohi became a pilot at age seventeen. Approached by WE!-Women Empowerment Expedition, which seeks to shatter global, cultural, and gender barriers, to attempt this dangerous flight in a smaller aircraft, Aarohi took on the mission. Pandit held a light sport pilot license, commercial license, and an instrument rating. The Mumbai pilot began her flight in a Pipestrel Sinus 912. Along the way, she set a number of world aviation records for women-first to fly solo across the Atlantic and Pacific Oceans in a LSA. At age 23, Aarohi touched down in 24 countries with her inspiring example of "can do." Interestingly, according to BBC News as reported in November 2018, Indian airlines employ the highest proportion of female pilots at 12.4%. That's according to the latest statistics from the International Society of Women Airline Pilots (ISWAP).

Parrish, Marie Odean "Deanie" Bishop
"Over 65 years ago, we each served our country without any expectations of recognition or glory, and we did it without compromising the values we were taught as we grew up: honor, integrity, patriotism, service, faith, and commitment. We did it because our country needed us. All we ever asked for is that our overlooked history no longer be a missing chapter in the history of World War II, the history of aviation, and the history of our country." Spoken March 10, 2010 in Washington, D.C., at the long awaited recognition of the incredible service of the Women Airforce Service Pilots of World War II with the awarding of the Congressional Gold Medal. WASP Deanie Parrish accepted this award on behalf of the WASP corps. At age 21, Deanie joined the WASP, serving first as an engineering test pilot at Greenville AFB. Later, she towed targets for new military men to learn how to shoot down airplanes from the ground…the men were using live ammunition.

(WASP "Deanie" Bishop Parrish. Creative Commons photograph.)

Parrish, Nancy
"No doubt the WASP blazed the trail for women serving as military pilots today, but for me, discovering these remarkable women and their stories has always been about so much more than flying. It is about living a life beyond what is expected, about being willing to risk stretching the boundaries and busting through the barriers. It is about doing what you feel is right, even when no one is looking and 'flying higher' in everything you do. That is not just history, it is inspirational history." Written in 2012, issue 21, *PilotMAG,* "Women of the WASP: The Fly Girls of WWII" by Nancy Parrish, daughter of WASP Deanie Parrish. Nancy is the author of *WASP In their Own Words*, Director of Wings Across America, creator/designer of the Fly Girls Traveling WASP Exhibit, and creator of WASP on the web www.wingsacrossamerica.us/WASP/.

Pellegreno, Ann Holtgreen
"I wanted to be an inspiration to other adventurers and dreamers. I hope I accomplished that." Quoted in June 2107 *EAA Sport Aviation Magazine,* "Around the World in 30 minutes" by Jim Busha. In 1967, at age 30 with newly-minted flight instructor, commercial, and multi-engine ratings, Ann and her crew set off in a 30-year-old rebuilt Lockheed 10 Electra, to retrace the 30-year flight path of the Amelia Earhart ill-fated around the world attempt. On July 7, 1967, Pellegreno and crew landed their beautiful Lockheed on the Oakland, CA, runway, after successfully flying the 28,000 miles. Her book, *World Flight: The Earhart Trail,* shares the planning, excitement, and commitment required to continue the aviation legacy.

Penney, Heather "Lucky."
"We all have that capacity but we don't have to wait for history, that we can all do something that changes somebody else's life today. And it might be a minor kindness. It might be just having a little bit extra courage to do the right thing. Or overcoming our own fears again to do that thing that needs to be done." March 30, 2020 Good Morning America broadcast, "Herstory Lessons: Female pilot was prepared to give her life to stop the 9/11 attacks." Born into an aviation family, Penney is a third generation pilot. She earned her pilot license at age 18. In 1993, when military combat aviation slots opened to women, she joined the District of Columbia Air National Guard. Her fighter squadron gave her the nickname, "Lucky" because of her last name. On that CAVU Tuesday morning of 9/11/2001, when the al-Qaeda terrorists took over United Flight 93 to use it as a weapon to kill more Americans, the order was given to intercept that plane before it reached D.C. Heather Penney scrambled her F-16 fighter knowing this was possibly a one-way suicide mission. She was prepared to sacrifice her life to protect our nation. The heroic passengers and crew of Flight 93 fought for control of the airliner. That plane crashed in a Pennsylvania field killing all 44 on-board. Later, Penney served two combat tours in Iraq. Today, Heather Penney works in our aerospace industry. She chairs the

advisory Board of the EAA Women Soar Society to encourage women to join the aviation and aerospace community.

Petitt, Karlene
"We are the protagonists of our stories called life, and there is no limit to how high we can fly." Quoted from http://karlenepetitt.blogspot.com. Karlene is an International Airline Captain with seven Boeing type-ratings, an Airbus 330 type, 21 years of instructing, and an accomplished writer and speaker.

Phillips, Pam
"I love experiencing something new every day. It's never the same. Looking into the future, I want to be here and continue to work for as long as I can help aviation and be involved." Quoted in the May-June 2020 *Ninety-Nines* magazine, "Following a Different Flight Plan," by Janice Pelletti. Pam Phillips learned the FBO business from her dad. At age 13, every weekend she worked at the reception desk. After high school, flight lessons followed. Pam did attend college as a business major but was looking for a new direction. She switched to the Travel Institute of American, after only a year, she earned her travel agent certificate. Still interested in the FBO business, she decided to work in the Fixed Based Operation parts shop. Suddenly, the Tri-City Aviation office manager unexpectedly left that position. This new opportunity to run the office and learn more about the Fixed Based Operation were a perfect match for Pam. Twenty years as the owner and president of Tri-City Aviation, Pam Phillips landed at just the right airport.

Popova, Nadezhda
"I look up into the dark sky, close my eyes and picture myself as a girl at the controls of my bomber, and I think, 'Nadya, how on earth did you do it?' " Quoted on www.thelily.com/dubbed-the-night-witches-these-female-wwii-pilots-were-fierce-and-feared/.
The Lily News adapted this story from *Washington Post's* Michael S. Rosenwald March 1, 2019 story. Popova was a Soviet "Night Witch."

She flew 852 missions as a 19 year-old girl in the famed World War II 588th Night Bomber Regiment. On July 15, 2013, Nadya died at age 91. In 1941, Marina Raskova, the Soviet version of Amelia Earhart, formed the Night Bomber women combat pilots. Raskova was the most famous Aviatrix of Russia and the first woman pilot and navigator in the Russian Air Force. The brave Soviet women flew dangerous missions from 1941 to 1945. Their planes were bi-planes flown at night over the German lines. They had old, noisy planes. Often the engines used to conk out halfway through their missions, so they had to climb out on the wings mid-flight to restart the props. To stop Germans from hearing them and starting up their anti-aircraft guns, the women flew almost at ground level, glided down to German positions, dropped their bombs, restarted their engines in midair and flew like the wind. Their airplanes made a ghostly sound and the Germans called them the "Night Witches."

Potter, Susan
"Every time I walk into the hangar, I'm excited. The feeling takes me back to when I was younger. I remember seeing those big Gulfstream jets taxing around and thinking, 'Wow, will I ever get to fly something like that?'" Quoted in January/February 2019, WAI *Aviation For Women* magazine, "From Gliders to Bizjets," by Patrick Bell. Susan Potter is the first female international Captain for the John Deere Global Aviation Services in Moline, Illinois. Two Cessna Citation X business jets, the world's fastest civilian aircraft, along with a large Gulfstream 550 corporate plane are deployed to reach global customers. Potter was introduced to aviation while a student in Colorado Springs at our U.S. Air Force Academy. Then, during her second year, it happened. Enrolled in the glider training program, on her first solo, she was overwhelmed with the beautiful sights from the air. She realized that flying was what she wanted and needed to do with her life. She left the Academy to return to Central Michigan to earn her aviation credentials. She became a flight instructor. She flew charters serving Midwestern businesses. On one flight, she just happened to land her customer at the

airport in Moline. While waiting for her passengers to return, she drove over to the John Deere hangar with her resume. In 1998, after her interview, she joined the aviation team. As the say, "The rest is history."

Quimby, Harriet
"There is no reason why the aeroplane should not open up a fruitful occupation for women." Quoted at www.azquotes.com. On August 1, 1911, American Journalist Quimby earned Aero Club of America pilot license #37 becoming the first American woman to be licensed. Harriet joined the Moisant International Aviators Exhibition Team. The media dubbed her 'The Dresden China Aviatrix" because she was petite, pretty, fair-skinned, and a huge fan favorite. A major sponsor, Vin Fiz grape soda, promoted this legendary aviator in her purple satin flying suit which graced every label on the popular drink bottle. In September 1911, Harriet Quimby gracefully performed in that iconic purple flying outfit becoming the first woman to make a night flight over a crowd, flying at a then incredible 15,000 AGL. On April 16, 1912, Quimby became the first female pilot in the world to fly across the English Channel. Bold and beautiful, Harriet Quimby inspired many to fly.

(Harriet Quimby. Library of Congress archive)

Rhoads, Sarah

"Set specific goals, taking one day at a time yet having a long-term vision and plan. Hold yourself to high standards, collaborate, and support others." Quoted in March/April 2018 WAI *Aviation For Women* magazine, "Leadership Lessons," by Ksenia Weisz. Sarah comes to her director of aviation operations at Amazon Air from extensive experience in the U.S. Navy. By age seven, she knew her future was in aviation when she attended her first air show. She applied to both the U.S. Air Force Academy and the U.S. Naval Academy and was accepted at both. She chose Annapolis where she studied mechanical engineering and began her quest to naval carrier jet training. During her naval career, Rhoads flew the F/A-18F Super Hornet, with the famous Black Aces of the VFA-41 squadron. Sarah flew 37 combat missions in support of Operation Iraqi Freedom. After military service, she transitioned on to the Amazon team in various roles with increasing responsibilities. Amazon Air is the cargo airline exclusively for transporting Amazon packages. By 2021, Amazon Air is projected to have at least 70 cargo aircraft flying out of over 20 United States air gateways.

Rice, Judy

"I tell students, if I can do it, so can you! Do not compare yourself to others. So what if it takes you longer. Most importantly, focus, do the work, and don't give up." Quoted in the fall 2018 *National Council for Aviation and Space Education*, "NCASE President Steps Down to focus on Her Passion-Flight Instruction," by Kim Stevens. When Judy was in first grade, she announced to her teacher she wanted to fly. Her teacher told her, "Honey, you are a girl. Good girls do not fly." Devastated, she told her parents and they agreed with her teacher. Judy learned to keep her dream of flying a secret. After graduating from college and years teaching in a special education classroom, her nine-year-old son bought her a flight lesson because she had shared her secret with him. She had to build the confidence in herself that she could indeed fly after a lifetime of being told aviation wasn't what "good girls" did. Her story reminds of Alicia Keys anthem song, "Girl on Fire," because by then

Judy's head was in the clouds and she was "balls to the wall!" Then, after ten years of planning, in 2015, Rice flew a Citation Mustang around the world, "Think Global Flight," to promote the importance of "STEAM-Science, Technology, Engineering, Art and Math" She is a Certified Flight Instructor. Learn more at www.CaptainJudy.com.

Ride, Sally
"If we want scientists and engineers in the future, we should be cultivating the girls as much as the boys." In 1978, newly-minted Dr. Sally Ride, physicist, joined five other stellar women, Anna Fisher, Shannon Lucid, Judith Resnik, Rhea Seddon, and Kathy Sullivan in the first NASA astronaut class allowing women. On June 18, 1983, Sally Ride on the Challenger as a mission specialist became America's first woman in space. After another space mission and several years with NASA, Sally Ride returned to Stanford University. She co-founded the Sally Ride Science education company. She was inducted into the National Women's and National Aviation Halls of Fame.

(Astronaut Sally Ride. NASA photograph)

Roberts, Stacey

"I always dreamed of flying but never knew it would be human flight. Skydiving ignited a passion so deep the view of the world changed and opened my mind to all possibilities. There's nothing limiting one's ability to achieve the unimaginable when you are freed by flight." Stacey, an experienced skydiver, is one of the 13 members of the premier Misty Blues (www.MistyBlues.net), an all-woman sky diving team who have been thrilling audiences since the early 1980s. In North America, about 35,000 enjoy this exciting sport. Only 13% of them are women. Misty Blues members also have full-time careers where they are highly successful professionals. The team has a few engineers, financial controller, welding instructor, airport manager, supply chain analyst, the list of accomplishments are amazing. Hobbies outside of skydiving range from pilot, rock climbing, running, glass blowing, and wood working. One of the favorite parts of performing is to walk into the crowd and meet many of the fans and inspire the next generation of aviators and skydivers. An inspiring, short video of Misty Blues team member, Cindy Irish, performing to our National Anthem with a 60-foot American Flag proudly waving from her foot at the 2013 Thunder Over Michigan Air Show is at www.youtube.com/watch?v=8v0i3NjOiBQ.

Robertson, Rebekah

"After a flight one day, a passenger in the cabin gave me a note as she was leaving the airplane. It said, 'thanks for a great and safe flight. You represent what strong, intelligent women should be.' And she wasn't a pilot either." Quoted in July 12, 2019, *Flying* (www.flyingmag.com) "Rebekah Robertson: Upgrading to Captain," by Rob Mark. In 2014, Robertson began her aviation journey in a Cessna 172 with her first flying lesson. Just a few short years later, she worked her way through the ratings and built the required hours to earn her right seat in a Trans States Airlines Embraer as First Officer. After nearly 1,100 flight hours, she transitioned to the coveted left seat as Captain. Now, with four strips as Captain and an additional 350 hours left-seat hours in her log book, she has set her next career goal of flying for United Airlines. Rebekah's story reminds me of the adage. *"A river cuts through a rock, not because of its power but its persistence."* Goal setting is an important component of successful aviation and aerospace careers.

Ross, Mary Golda

"I was the only female in my class. I sat on one side of the room and the guys on the other side of the room. I guess they didn't want to associate with me. But I could hold my own with them, and sometimes did better." https://todayinsci.com/R/Ross_Mary/RossMary-Quotations.htm. In 2019, Ross was inducted into the Women In Aviation International Pioneer Hall of Fame. She is our first known Native American female Lockheed Corporation engineer. From 1942 until retirement in 1973, she was one of just 40 founding engineers of the highly secretive and renowned "Skunk Works." She is best remembered for her work on aerospace designs, Agena Rocket program, interplanetary space travel, Earth-orbiting flight, and satellites. In 2018, Ross was chosen to be depicted on the 2019 Native American $1 Coin by the U.S. Mint celebrating American Indians in the space program. She was a proud member of the Cherokee Nation.

Rovner, Sarah

"I want to share my passion for aviation with others and promote aviation in every way I can." Sarah is founder and CEO of FullThrottle Aviation, an International aircraft delivery and handling company. This unique company can ferry aircraft and also provide advanced flight instruction to a new aircraft owner on the ferry flight home. Sarah has assembled a team of aviation professionals to deliver airplanes around the world, including oceanic crossings. Since changing careers from a network engineer in the oil and gas industry to aviation full time, she has flown over 140 different types of airplanes and built-up 6,000 hours of flight time. She holds an ATP, CFI, CFII, MEI, and licenses in four countries (USA, Canada, Belize, and Iceland-EASA). In addition to being a FAA Safety Team Lead representative and FAA Gold Seal CFI, she also earned the National Association of Flight Instructor-NAFI

Master Instructor Accreditation for the second time. Sarah Rovner is following her passion and creating a new generation of confident pilots. Her blog is https://fullthrottleaviation.wordpress.com.

Roz, Ellen
"My advice for women who are considering aviation-whether a career or just for fun-is to surround yourself with positive, enthusiastic people." Quoted in May/June 20019 *Aviation for Women*, "Women of Emirates," by Abigail Welch. Captain Roz commands a Boeing 777 for the Dubai-based airline, Emirates. She came from an aviation family and knew from an early age her goal was commercial aviation. She completed flight training in Tulsa, OK. Then was hired as a Flight Instructor at the same school. She kept her focus on building experience, flight hours, and networking.

Rutherford, Linda
"My mother told me I could be anything I wanted to be if I believed in myself, never gave up, and gave 110 percent to everything." Quoted on Southwest Airline corporate web site. Rutherford is Senior Vice President and Chief Communications Office at the airline. She began her career in corporate communications and outreach with a Journalism degree. In 1992, Rutherford joined Southwest Airlines team and over the years has served in several key positions. She has earned numerous awards to include Business Woman of the Year and joined several Halls of Fame to include PR News Public Relations and the Texas Tech College of Mass Communications. She is often listed as one of the top women champions of communications.

Safety is not a device. It is a state of mind. ~ Unknown

8
S-Sierra to U-Uniform

Take quiet time to reflect daily because these moments give way to clarity and direction. ~ Unknown

Serbinenko, Anna

"My message to girls out there is that, YES, you can learn to fly, that, YES, you can achieve anything if you set your mind to it. Look at me. I didn't start flying until I got to Canada in 2009 and now I'm flying aerobatics before big crowds across North America." Quoted in August 22, *2016 AOPA Aviation eBrief*, "Pilot Spotlight." Serbinenko was born in Ukraine. She became a Swiss banker. Later, she moved to Canada. Now, Anna is an aerobatic airshow performer, who flies an American Super Decathlon in her choreographed, graceful sky dance to classical music. Her web site is www.annaskydancer.com.

Shotwell, Gwynne

"I was inspired to become an engineer by a very smart, well-dressed mechanical engineer who I saw speak at a Society of Women Engineers event as a teenager. She was doing really critical work and I loved her suit. That's what a 15-year-old girl connects with. I used to shy away from telling that story, but if that's what caused me to be an engineer, I think we should talk about that." Quoted on June 21, 2018 *Fortune's* "The 39 most powerful female engineers of 2018," at www.BusinessInsider.com. Shotwell is COO of Space X. In 2018, she was inducted into the Space and Satellite Hall of Fame. She is ranked Number 1 on *Fortune's* 2018 Most Powerful Female Engineers List.

Shults, Tammie Jo

"I think none of us break through a barrier all by ourselves. The WASPs (Women Airforce Service Pilots) didn't demand to get to fly. They simply were needed. They nudged a door open. If Rosemary Mariner and the other ladies in the first class (of female aviators) had done poorly, the doors would not have been opened for the rest of us to get a chance to fly. Everyone given an opportunity has the obligation to make sure the trail they open is opened properly for those coming behind them. The doors that women pushed open, many of them were unlocked by men-proving we have always worked best when we work together." Quoted in March 2020 *Military Officer Magazine,* "Fly like a Girl." Tammie Jo was the Navy's first female F/A-18 Hornet pilot. In the early 1990s, she joined Southwest Airlines. She worked to reach Captain. On April 17, 2018, she was pilot-in-command of Flight 1380, a Boeing 737, when the airliner experienced catastrophic engine failure, explosion, severe aircraft fuel line and hydraulic damages. Captain Shults met the challenge, landed the plane safely, and saved the lives of 148 people.

Silitch, Mary

"Get all the experience you can. Don't let anyone tell you that you can't." Quoted in May 2014 *AOPA Pilot* magazine, "Mary Silitch: An Aviation Journalism Pioneer," by Benet Wilson. Time after time in her legendary career, Mary faced gender discrimination. But, she kept doing her best until a new door opened. Mary fell in love with aviation at age four, flying in a crop-duster over her family's Arkansas farm. As a young woman with a college degree in journalism, New York City was her destination. In 1965, after *Mademoiselle,* the *Saturday Evening Post,* and McGraw-Hill Book Company, associate editor at *Flying* magazine opened up with flight lessons as an additional benefit. In 1969, Mary left because she was told she would never become *Flying* managing editor…because she was a girl. *Air Progress* offered Mary their managing editor position. More opportunities opened up, some of Mary's own making because she knew she could do the job well. Positions at AOPA, Seaplane Pilots, *Aero* magazine, *Private Pilot,*

Professional Pilot, and *Aviation International News,* all benefited from Mary's immense writing talents. In 2013, Mary Silitch was inducted into the Women in Aviation International Hall of Fame.

Simi, Bonnie

"You have to have a dream for a dream to come true." Quoted on *www.JetBlueVentues.com.* Simi is President of JetBlue Technology Ventures. She is a former JetBlue airline captain and three-time Luge Olympian with extensive corporate and broadcast experience.

Sindelar, Teresa

"I used to climb out of my window and sit on the roof, much to my mother's dismay, to look at stars." Quoted in the spring, 2017 *Nebraska Magazine,* "Fulfilling Her Space Dream,' by Kelly Riibe. Sindelar began her journey as a teenage "space camper" at the Cosmosphere in Hutchinson, Kansas. After multiple summers, from 1998 to 2010, Teresa became a counselor, intern, and full-time staffer. Now, an environmental health systems crew instructor for NASA, she trains astronauts on earth. Sindelar earned her undergraduate degree in Geology and geosciences. She earned her Masters in Curriculum and Instruction. She shared her enthusiasm and talent in the high school classroom. Her NASA instructional role gives her an opportunity to feel like she contributing to our space exploration.

Skelton, Betty Frankman Erde

"Competing? No, I didn't really do that. I found that once I demonstrated I was capable, had the ability, I was accepted. And I found that true everywhere I've ever been and in everything I've ever done." Quoted at www.airandspace.si.edu. Betty was an exceptional pilot and automobile test driver. She has more combined records than any other woman in history. For three years in a row, 1948, 1949, and 1950, she was the Feminine International Aerobatic Champion. She became the first woman to perform an inverted ribbon cut only ten feet above the ground. In 1949, she set the world light plane altitude record of 25,763 feet in a Piper Cub. In 1951, she set another Piper Cub altitude record of 29,050 feet. She set the World Speed Record for a P-51 racing plane over a 3km course at 421.6 mph. In 1959, the Mercury 7 Astronauts nicknamed her 7 ½ because she completed the same physical and psychological tests they took. Her red and white Pitts Special, named "Little Stinker," hangs at the Smithsonian Air & Space Museum, upside down, of course. In 1997, Betty became a Women in Aviation International Pioneer Hall of Fame member. In 2005, she was inducted into the National Aviation Hall of Fame.

(Elinor Smith 1942. Library of Congress archival photograph)

Smith, Elinor

"It had long since come to my attention that people of accomplishment rarely sat back and let things happen to them. They went out and happened to things." Quote from www.brainyquote.com. In 1928, she flew a Waco 10 under all four New York City East River bridges, creating celebrity status and earning her the nickname, "The Flying Flapper of Freeport." She continued a record-setting aviation career as the first female test pilot for both Fairchild and Bellanca aircraft companies. In 2001, Women in Aviation International honored Elinor in their Pioneer Hall of Fame.

Snyder, Heather

"It is important to me that people understand success in aviation is not instant nor is it guaranteed. This is a career where success depends largely on your willingness to play the long game and manage setbacks that are beyond your control." Heather's words in May-June 2019 *Ninety-Nines* magazine, "I kept My Eyes on the Prize for 20 Years." Now, Captain Snyder at a major airline, she began her training in 1998. She became the first woman to graduate in the Utah Valley State College flight training program. Without a mentor, it was a lonely journey sometimes. Over the years, the airlines hit with 9/11 terrorism furloughed many of their talented crew members during the slowdowns in travel. Heather was one of them so she looked for airline opportunity with foreign carriers until she could navigate back to United. Over the years, training and more training helped with the turbulence in the airline industry. Captain Heather Snyder is now type rated in the EMB145, A320, B737, B757/767, B777, and B747.

Stamats, Susan

"I've had so many incredible experiences flying. I've flown on several different continents and flown over the Rocky Mountains, but every flight is different. I still feel it's magical just to fly over my home town." Quoted August 7, 2012 *News-Journal* (Longview TX), "Women balloon pilots enjoy competitions, life in the skies," by Angela Ward. In

1977, Stamats began balloon crewing. By 1984, Susan became a licensed balloon pilot. She competed in several U.S. National Hot Air Balloon Championships. Women in the early 1800s, flew various hot air balloons. France's Madame Sophie Blanchard is often credited as being the first woman to fly solo. On June 16, 1934, Jeannette Piccard became the first in America. Later, she set high altitude records that stood for decades.

Stenbock, Natasha

"Failures or decisions that didn't turn out just lead you to the next path. I have no regrets, even if things weren't perfect." Quoted in July-August 2020 *Ninety-Nines* magazine, "Natasha Stenbock Transformed Fear to Empowerment," by Lauren Nagel, Montreal Chapter. Natasha, as an American Meteorological Society (AMS) Chief Meteorologist for KOIN6 News in Oregon, wanted to stop being afraid. To overcome her fear of flying, she marched to her local flight school counter and signed up for lessons. Ground school gave her the understanding she desperately needed to understand the science of flying and the phenomena that had previously baffled and frightened her. That understanding grew to empowerment. After earning her private pilot certificate, she continued on to complete her IFR rating with some bumps along the way for her written test. Persistence has paid off in aviation and in her career.

Stofan, Ellen

"If you can't see it, you can't be it. We want to make sure we are giving girls examples of female pilots and aircraft designers..." Quoted in November/December 2018 WAI *Aviation For Women,* "Leading a National Treasure," by Kelly Murphy. Dr. Ellen Stofan is inspiring the revitalization of our iconic Smithsonian Air and Space Museum. Somewhat of a "homecoming" for Stofan, who was a student intern at that museum. Now, with more than 25 years of space-related organizational experience and deep planetary geology research background, she loves science and space. During her post-doctoral fellowship at NASA's Jet Propulsion Laboratory and as chief scientist, long-range visions are always on the horizon. Sending humans to Mars and even beyond can be imagined. Now firmly on the ground at the Smithsonian but eyes always fixed on space, Ellen Stofan wants women to continue to play a significant role.

Sullivan, Kathryn D. "Kathy"

(NASA Kathryn D Sullivan. NASA photograph)

"I was always interested in exploring. Maps and landscapes appeal to me and I have always had a desire to explore. When I was growing up, we as a nation were involved in two grand adventures: the space program and underwater exploration. I was fascinated by both." Quoted from summer 2005, *Association for Women in Science Magazine.* Sullivan is a former astronaut, National Oceanic & Atmospheric Administration Administrator, and the first women to fly in space and descend to the deepest point in the ocean which she did on June 7, 2020. In 1979, she became an astronaut. In 1984, Sullivan became the first American women to walk in space and is a veteran of three space flights. As a private pilot, she flies a Super Decathlon. In 2010, Dr. Sullivan joined other Sky Stars in the Women in Aviation International Pioneer Hall of Fame.

Swegle, Madeline "Maddy"

"After three years, that was a long journey and there were times I did not think I would make it. That was scary. But, I am glad I kept pushing." Quoted on August 24, 2020 Military.com original video by Austin Rooney (Navy), "Sky's The Limit; Meet Maddy Swegle, Navy's First Black Female Tactical Jet Pilot." Forty years after Brenda E. Robinson became the Navy's first African American female naval aviator, women in military aviation continue to blaze trails. Swegle is doing so in the Navy's most advanced aircraft. Lt. j.g. Swegle is a graduate of the U.S. Naval Academy and trained in the T-45c Goshawk jet trainer aircraft.

If plan 'A' doesn't work, always have a back-up plan because you still have 25 more letters left in the alphabet to use for your new plan to reach the stars. ~Unknown

(U.S. Navy Pilot Madeline Swegle. U.S. Navy photograph)

Talen-Keller, Ariel

"I love participating in missions for Civil Air Patrol and love the camaraderie with the aviation crowd. CAP is a group of great people sharing a common passion and interest and using it to help others." Quoted in the April-June 2013, *Civil Air Patrol Volunteer* magazine, "Aero Femme: Mrs. Alaska United America serves as role model for female cadets," by Jennifer S. Kornegay. As part of her platform as the reigning Mrs. Alaska U.S. All World Beauties 2012, Ariel adopted the inspiring theme, "GirlsFlyToo!" message to encourage and educate women of all ages to join the aviation industry. In 2010, she founded Aero Femme, a non-profit with the mission to encourage and educate women of all ages to be involved in all aspects of aviation. Aero Femme provides scholarships and promotes aviation career opportunities for women. Growing up on an Oregon private airfield with pilot parents, aviation as a business was a natural path. After flight school at the prestigious University of North Dakota's John D. Odegard School of Aerospace Sciences, Ariel earned her Embrey-Riddle aeronautical sciences Master's degree. In addition to flying, she trained in air traffic control. In aviation and aerospace, women already have "the right stuff." They need to see these outstanding role models early and often.

Tereshkova, Valentina

"One cannot deny the great role women have played in the world community. My flight was yet another impetus to continue female contribution." Quoted on www.BrainyQuote.com. In 1963, she became the first and youngest woman in the world to fly in space on a solo mission. In Vostok 6, Valentina, as a Russian Cosmonaut, she orbited the earth 48 times, spent almost three days in space, and remains the only woman on earth to have been on a successful, solo space mission.

Thaden, Louise McPhetridge

"Flight is the essence of the spirit. It nurtures the soul. It is awesome. Often ethereal. Glorious. Emotionally wondrous and all-pervading. Intangible." Louise Thaden's words in her autobiography, *High, Wide and Frightened.* Stellar aviation pioneer, Thaden set numerous aviation records. In 1928, she set the women's altitude record of 20,260 feet. In March 1929, she set the women's endurance record of 22 hours, 3 minutes, 12 seconds. In 1936, Louise became the first woman to win the coveted Bendix Trophy. She is a charter member of the Ninety-Nines. In 1951, Bentonville AR, honored her legacy by renaming their airport, Louise Thaden Field. In 1999, Thaden was enshrined in the National Aviation Hall of Fame. In 2000, she joined the Women in Aviation International Pioneer Hall of Fame.

Twining, Kristie

"Women excel in aviation. We can do anything with hard work, very hard work at times. If you are willing to do that, I tell them [young girls] the sky is the limit. Only you can stop yourself. If you want something, you have to work hard for it. Put your mind and heart 110% into your goals, and never ever ever give up." Quoted in November/December WAI *Aviation For Women* magazine, "NOAA Way," by Mary Walsh. National Oceanic and Atmospheric Administration (NOAA) is a federal agency focused on enriching life through science. Everything from daily weather monitoring and forecasts, severe storm warnings, fishery management, coastal restoration, and support for marine commerce are provided. NOAA Commissioned Officer Corps includes several dedicated women aviators for the NOAA fleet. Kristie Twining started as an ensign on a survey vessel in Alaska waters. In 2002, she was accepted into the flight program. She has logged over 4,800 hours in the NOAA G-IV and Twin Otter flying hurricane missions and conducting atmospheric research. Commander Twining is an instructor pilot, G-IV aircraft commander, and is chief of the Aircraft Maintenance Branch. Another important role is to speak to women and young girls about aviation. Kristie Twining believes sharing NOAA opportunities will build a better future for everyone.

(NOAA photograph of hurricane hunters. Pilots left seat; LtCdr. Rebecca Waddington and right seat; CDR.Kristie Twining)

Underwood, Lindsay

"In aviation, there are so many alternatives, and gaining that experience through more experienced pilots or through flying in a multitude of aircraft allows you to see what is out there to get the job done." Quoted in the March/April 2019 *Ninety-Nines* magazine, "Lindsay Underwood and the President's Helicopter," by Jacqueline Boyd. The Sikorsky VH-92A will replace an aging fleet of Presidential helicopters. Lindsay is the first female pilot to command the U.S. President's elite new military transport helicopter for the U.S. Marine Corps. After serving in several helicopter squadrons, Lindsay became a U.S. Navy Test Pilot, before joining this new role. In addition to flying, Lindsay will be the Platform Coordinator for the Presidential Helicopter Program which flies not only the President and Vice-President, Heads of State, Department of Defense officials and any others directed by the Marine Corps and White House Military Office. All part of her busy day as a new mother. In fact, Lindsay logged about 50 hours in a Sikorsky MH-60R Seahawk while pregnant with Alice, a future Ninety-Nine just like Mom!

(SWA Ramp Agent secures luggage. Courtesy of Southwest Airlines.)

9
V-Victor to Z-Zulu

Keep Calm and Fly On
~ Unknown

Vacher, Polly

"Before I had more time to think, we launched into space. After the initial unwelcomed feeling of freefalling, I was overcome with the most exhilarating sense of peace and wonder. Once at terminal velocity of 120 mph, the sensation of falling disappeared and I was flying like a bird. The clouds puffed around us and amazingly I could use my arms and legs to move about. I was filled with an unimaginable sense of awe. From that moment there was no looking back." Polly describing her first skydiving experience for charity in her book, *Wings Around the World: The Exhilarating Story of One Woman's Epic Flight from the North Pole to Antarctica.* In 1994, Polly was 50 years old when she earned her pilot's license with her husband while they lived in Australia. In 2001, Vacher successfully flew her Piper Cherokee on a solo eastbound circumnavigation of the world for charity to fund flying scholarships for the disabled in Great Britain. Polly's Wings Around the World Challenge earned worldwide support. In 2003, flying for that same charity, she set out on a "Voyage to the Ice," flying over the North Pole, Antarctica, and all seven continents, becoming the first solo woman pilot to fly over the polar ice caps in a single-engine plane.

Van Ovost, Jacqueline D.

"Don't let anyone tell you that you can't do it. It's that imposter syndrome (mentality), the small voice that you think you have in your head that says, 'You're not good enough, and even though some other person has done it, you are not as good as they are.' It's real and it can be paralyzing." Quoted September 13, 2020, *Military.com*, "She Once Was Barred from Fighter Jets. Now She's the Pentagon's Only Female Four Star," by Oriana Pawlyk. In 1988, Van Ovost graduated from the U.S. Air Force Academy when the Pentagon policy prohibited women from flying in combat. In 1993, when that ban was lifted, Van Ovost immediately pursued reassignment as a test pilot at Edwards Air Force Base flying A-10 Thunderbolt II and the first iteration of the C-17 cargo plane, now considered the backbone of Air Force airlift operations. General Jacqueline Van Ovost fondly remembers the morning of June 18, 1983, flying her father's Cessna 172 Skyhawk in a holding pattern outside of Cape Canaveral in anticipation of the historic NASA mission where Sally Ride became our first American woman in space. Proudly wearing her "Ride, Sally, Ride!" blue t-shirt, she has kept that t-shirt all these years as a reminder of those who "broke the glass ceilings of air and space." General Van Ovost feels her mission is to continue blazing those trails and widen the trails for the future.

Wagstaff, Patty

"The Sky represents Adventure, Freedom, and Challenge." Quoted on her web site www.PattyWagstaff.com. Daughter of a Japan Airlines pilot, Patty began her flying adventures early. In Alaska, she earned single, multi-engine, seaplane, commercial, and instrument ratings. Then, she qualified for Certified Flight and Instrument Instructor ratings. Later, she earned a commercial rotorcraft rating. In 1985, she joined the United States National Aerobatic Team. In 1991, Patty Wagstaff won her first of three U.S. National Aerobatic Championships. In 1993, she won the International Aerobatic Club Champion title. From 1988 to 1994, Patty won the Betty Skelton First Lady of Aerobatics Award, an amazing six times in a row. In 1997, Women in Aviation

International inducted Patty into their Pioneer Hall of Fame. In 2004, she was elected to the National Aviation Hall of Fame. In 2005, Patty received the Katharine Wright Award.

(Patty Wagstaff. Courtesy photograph Patty Wagstaff.)

Waiz, Shaesta

"Every time I open the door to an aircraft, I ask myself, 'How did a girl with my background become so lucky?' The truth is, anyone can be me. **You must believe in yourself and allow your dreams to soar.**" Quoted on www.DreamsSoar.org. Shaesta is the first certified civilian female pilot from Afghanistan, graduating with bachelors and master's degrees from Embry Riddle Aeronautical University. In 1987, her family made the long journey from Afghanistan to America as war refugees. She is the youngest pilot to fly solo around the world in a single-engine airplane.

Warner, Emily Howell

"Flying was so important to me, I was willing to sacrifice the things that young people normally buy with their hard-earned wages. No records, ice cream, movies. It was a struggle at first...Flying lessons were $12.75 an hour. I had to pay $20 a week for room and board at home. As a retail clerk at the department store, I probably only made $50 a week. But, I loved flying and was determined." Quoted in March 2001 *Colorado County Life*, "On the Wings of Dreams: Colorado Woman takes Flight." According to the National Aviation Hall of Fame, Emily built her flight experience even ferrying new Cessna 150's from Wichita back to Denver with no radios installed. In 1960, she became a flight instructor, and was soon promoted to flight school manager and chief pilot. Over time Emily upgraded her aviation ratings, enabling her to provide flight instruction to the many airline pilots – all males. She applied to the airlines for a pilot's job, but even with her 7,000 hours, the industry was not ready for a woman airline pilot. The fact that less qualified male students she was instructing were being hired by the airlines was not lost on her. Determined, Warner persisted, routinely, and politely making her interest known to anyone in the offices of the airlines. By 1973, after seven years of trying, when Emily was not selected for the new airline hiring class of pilots, she marched into the Frontier office and landed an interview with the airlines' Vice President of Flight Operations, Ed O'Neil. Even with her outstanding qualification, Frontier made Emily prove she could fly by putting her in the flight simulator. She clearly showed them how well she could fly. She was hired. Emily and Frontier airlines made aviation history. Emily believed her role was to mentor and encourage women in aviation and the airlines. She is a charter member of the International Society of Women Airline Pilots (ISA+21). After Frontier, Emily flew for Continental Airlines, and United Parcel Service (UPS). In 1990, she joined the

Federal Aviation Administration (FAA) as a Flight Examiner. Emily was the FAA Aircrew Program Manager for United Airlines Boeing 737 fleet. During her career she flew over 21,000 hours and conducted over 3,000 check rides. She earned the FAA Wright Brother's Award. Highly respected, Emily was inducted into the Colorado Aviation Hall of Fame (1983), Women in Aviation International Pioneer Hall of Fame (1992), National Women's Hall of Fame (2001), Colorado Women's Hall of Fame (2002), and included in the Living Legends of Aviation and the National Aviation Hall of Fame (2014), along with many other important awards and recognitions for her contributions to aviation history. On July 2015, her home airport in Granby, Colorado, was named Emily Warner Field.

Waye, Denise
"Just because it's hard, it doesn't mean you can't do it. If you really believe in something, follow your dream. There will be many naysayers who will tell you something can't be done, but say to yourself, 'Just watch me! I can do this!'" Quoted in March/April 2020 *Aviation For Women* magazine, "Taking the Untraditional Path: Nurse turned pilot, Denise Waye provides critical care services in the air."

Weeks, Samantha
"Many people will hold back from trying something for fear of failure. They won't fail, but they won't succeed and reach their full potential." As Colonel Weeks told Kathryn McNutt in winter 2020 *Sooner Magazine*, "OU alumna a real-life 'Captain Marvel' as U.S. Air Force pilot and base commander." As the daughter of an Air Force master sergeant, Samantha knew from any early age she wanted to be a fighter pilot. She was told early and often that "girls don't do that." In 1993, when Weeks entered the U.S. Air Force Academy, Congress decided that "Girls COULD do that." After graduation in 1997, she completed F-15C Eagle fighter jet training. Over time, Samantha built up 2,200 flying hours with 105 of those in combat/combat support. Then, in 2007, the dream aviator job of U.S. Air Force Thunderbird aerial

demonstration team member became hers. Even in this new century, as one of America's Ambassadors in Blue, she would hear the comment, "I didn't know women could do that." Leadership has always been an important part of military training. Since 2018, Colonel Weeks commands the 14th Flying Training Wing with full responsibility for operations, training, maintenance, budgeting, and managing 400 pilots, support for 244 aircraft, and keeping on time and on budget.

Wells, Stephanie
"My aviation role models are Jacqueline Cochran and Amelia Earhart because they were real women. They both accomplished things no one else had done before. They were amazing examples of what success is like, if you focus on your goal." Retired Air Force Lt. Colonel Wells discovered the joy of aviation in high school as a cadet in the Civil Air Patrol. In college, she earned her private pilot license, while carrying a full course load and working part-time. In 1975, with a meteorology degree with an Air Force Second Lieutenant commission, she entered active duty as a weather officer. On weekends to keep flying, she held a part-time job as a tow plane pilot for gliders. Just a few years later, Wells joined the third class of female pilot trainees at Williams AFB in Arizona. She earned a slot after graduation as a T-37 flight instructor. She continued to take advantage of every training and upgrade opportunity for advanced ratings and qualifications. During Desert Storm, Stephanie flew the Air Force C5 Galaxy on worldwide missions. In 1986, NASA gave her the opportunity to join their team as a staff pilot. Working with senior staff and astronauts provided a dynamic aviation and aerospace environment. In 2003, she left NASA to join the Denver office of the Federal Aviation Administration. Passionate about aviation and environment, Stephanie volunteered for LightHawk. She flew a number of missions. A frequent participant in the annual Air Race Classic, Stephanie is a constant presence in the Colorado 99s. Stephanie Wells is a highly qualified aviator with Air Transport Pilot, Certified Flight Instructor and Certified Flight Instructor Instrument, along with

Multi-Engine Instrument ratings, who shares her talent to build a new generation of women in air and space.

(Stephanie Wells. Penny Hamilton photographer.)

Welsh, Doreen

"What would you do if you only had '90 Seconds to (make an) Impact?'" Quoted from her Aviation Speakers Bureau and YouTube programs about her experience and lessons learned as a 38-year veteran flight attendant on the "Miracle on the Hudson." At 58-years old, Doreen had trained and trained again for this situation. In 2010, on US Airways Flight 1549, she heroically evacuated her passengers from the badly damaged rear of the plane which crashed on the Hudson River at 150 mph after geese hit the engines and disabled the plane. Normally, flight attendants are trained to evacuate passengers from the rear of the plane. Now, with that part of the aircraft quickly filling with icy water, Doreen badly hurt and bleeding in the crash landing, knew exactly what to do and say to move her passengers to safety on the wings for rescue by boats. Now retired from the airlines and a professional speaker, she urges listeners to reflect on the important people in our lives and tell them that often. To know that each of us has a "survivor instinct" to use when needed. To value training and team work as she credits flight attendants, Donna Dent and Sheila Dale with saving the lives of all 150 passengers and to the aviation skills of Captain "Sully" Sullenberger and co-pilot, Jeff Skiles. Always remember, "If the heart of airplane is the engine. The flight crew is the brain."

Wiatt, Katie McIntire
"I was just really struck with her skill (National Aerobatic Champion, Patty Wagstaff) and what she was accomplishing, so I started researching a little bit more about her. I realized I didn't know much about it and so certainly there had to be other people out there who didn't know much, as well. I wanted to make a documentary to tell people about what women are doing today and what women have done in aviation history." *Fly Like A Girl* feature-length documentary director quoted on April 16, 2019 www.baynews9.com.

Wilson, Emily
"Flying is something I really love, and I feel so excited and blessed at the opportunity to turn this into a career. I would tell any young girl out there that wants to learn to fly, but may be doubting themselves, that you are fully capable if you set your mind to it!" A twin who earned her private pilot certificate on the same day as her sister, Lexie. Quoted from "A Twin Achievement," *Flying* (flyingmag.com) by Julie Boatman, January 9, 2020. Emily is pursuing a career in the airline industry.

Wilson, Heather
"It's hard to be what you can't see." Quoted September 16, 2020 *FlightGlobal*, "The former U.S. Air Force Secretary leading the push for more women to take flight," by Pilar Wolfsteller. Wilson was commenting on the low numbers of females in the aviation industry. As the leader of the new Women in Aviation Advisory Board (WIAAB) established in the 2018 FAA re-authorization bill, Wilson leads an outstanding team of 30 female aviation industry professionals to develop strategies to reverse the lower numbers. An instrument-rated

private pilot and owner, Wilson, president of a University, came to aviation early. Her grandfather was an early barnstormer. Her father a commercial pilot. As one of the first women admitted to the United States Air Force Academy, Wilson excelled. She was the first woman to serve as Vice Wing Commander. In 1982, she became a Distinguished Graduate and earned a Rhodes scholarship. At Oxford, Wilson published the award-winning book, *International Law and the Use of Force by National Liberation Movements*. Heather Wilson, while serving in the Air Force, was a negotiator, NATO planner, and political advisor. Later, she was elected to Congress several times. In 2017, she was appointed Secretary of the Air Force. A strong voice for women in leadership, Heather Wilson and her WIAAB members will provide a wealth of ideas to continue to build our future national aviation and aerospace workforce.

Wilson, Lexie
"What initially inspired me to get into aviation was my dad and his career…He has been able to show me firsthand what life in the cockpit is like. I remember how happy he would be coming home from work, and—no matter the time of day—always had a huge grin on his face. I knew he was doing something he loved, and I wanted to make sure to find something that made me smile just like he did." A twin who earned her private pilot certificate on the same day as her sister, Emily. Quoted from "A Twin Achievement," *Flying* (flyingmag.com) by Julie Boatman, January 9, 2020. Lexie is pursuing an airline career.

Wilson, Stephanie
"When I was about thirteen I was given a school assignment in a Career Awareness class to interview someone that worked in the career field in which I was interested. I interviewed a local area astronomy professor. I thought that astronomy was a fantastic career, being able to teach, being able to see events in the heavens, and to do the observations. Later, I became more interested in engineering and decided that I would study engineering in college and perhaps that aerospace engineering

would be a good combination of my interests in astronomy and my interest in engineering." Quoted in a NASA interview on March 8, 2010. In 1996, she was selected for the astronaut programs, making Stephanie the second Black American female in the space program.

(Stephanie Wilson. NASA photograph.)

Wise, Lucile Doll

"I'm so impressed by what women pilots are doing today, especially flying into combat. They are doing some great flying and proving once again that women can fly military aircraft as well as men." Quoted March 2, 2016 *DOD News Features*, "Female World War II pilot Proud to be a WASP," by Shannon Collins. In May 1943, Wise joined the WASP with 50 hours of flight time. On December 20, 1944, when the federal government disbanded the WASP, Wise had flown almost 700 hours in the effort to win World War II. From 1942 to 1944, America's WASP flew over 60 million miles is support of our military effort. They towed targets behind their planes for men on the ground to learn how to use their weapons with live ammo. WASP flew every type of U.S. military aircraft to include the B-26 and B-29 bombers. They ferried new aircraft from factories and planes recently repaired back to useful service. They flew countless domestic flights for our military and civilian leaders. Thirty-eight WASP died during their World War II service.

Wolfe, Kristin "BEO"

"A lot of people have [misconceptions] still about either females flying or females being fighter pilots, all the way from little kids…to adults. So that's probably the most important part, is that they get to see it…for them to see that anything's possible. The jet doesn't care if you're a male or female." Quoted July 31, 2020 *Military.com* "The Jet Doesn't Care: 1st Female F-35 Demo Pilot Says She's Focused on Excellence," by Oriana Pawlyk. Captain Kristin "Beo" Wolfe is the new face of the U.S. Air Force's F-35 Joint Strike Fighter demonstration team. One of a handful of skillful women F-35A stealth jet pilots. She is a former F-22 Raptor pilot. More women are considering the military option for flight careers.

Ziler, Lois Hollingsworth "Holly"

"We were trained to fly radio-controlled target planes from a mother ship. This was the earliest in drone target or drone flying." Quoted in *Texas Women in World War II* by Cindy Weigand about service as a WASP. In 1927, Holly was inspired by Lindbergh's Sprit of St. Louis flight. At only age seven, she began building airplane models with the boys. At age 11, she was orphaned and had to live with relatives. Very enterprising, she saved her baby-sitting money so that at age 16 she would solo in an open cockpit biplane, earning her license a year later. In high school she met Amelia Earhart who encouraged her to pursue engineering at Purdue. Holly did just that. In 1939, she graduated Cum

Laude with a mechanical aeronautics engineering degree. She was offered an aeronautical engineering position at United Aircraft in Hartford, CT. Holly earned $135/month which is about $2,500/month in 2020 dollars. The average wage for women in manufacturing was around $100/month. Holly continued aviation flight training, earning her commercial license. In 1943, Holly volunteered for the Women's Flying Training Detachment (WFTD), later renamed Women Airforce Service Pilots, in support of the War effort. After the deactivation of the WASP and a move to El Paso, TX, Holly conducted flight training. In 1946, she married one of her students, Doyle Ziler. Eventually, they moved to Dell City, TX, and farmed. She continued "living large in aviation" when she opened Holly's Flying School. On October 27, 2000, Holly earned her second set of wings when she flew west.

(1960s Trans-Canada Airline Air Hostesses show off for the camera.)

10
Potpourri

If you are going to fly high, you have to give up all the baggage weighing you down. ~ Anonymous

Much of the "romance" surrounding air and space is about the long traditions and special bonds. Here are a few to consider.

Several historic explanations exist for the origins of the word cockpit. Some say it evolved from an early 17th century nautical term, and, possibly, earlier reference to the enclosed area where cock fights were held. Others offer other historic possibilities. Eventually aviation adopted it because typically the airplane control area is small, enclosed, and the center of flight operations. The Royal Air Force began using the term "flight deck" to indicate the upper platform in the large "flying boats" where the pilot and co-pilot sat. Words are powerful. However, the airplane is gender neutral.

As early as 1903, Aida de Acosta from New Jersey was the first woman to pilot a motorized aircraft (dirigible) solo while on a trip to Paris. From 1909, important early firsts for women were: Katherine Wright, first woman to fly as a passenger with her brothers in France.

World's first woman to fly solo as the pilot, Baroness Raymonde de Laroche and she became the first woman licensed.

September 16, 1910, first American woman to fly solo, Bessica Raiche, although some historians credit Blanche Stuart Scott.

August 1, 1911, America's first licensed woman pilot, Harriet Quimby.

Not long after, on August 10, 1911, Russia's Lydia Zvereva became the first woman licensed in her county.

On June 21, 1913, Georgia "Tiny" Broadwick became the first woman to jump from on airplane. That same year, Katherine Stinson became our first woman pilot to fly the U.S. Mail and first woman to own a flying school and form an aviation company with her mother.

(Katherine Stinson. Library of Congress archival photograph)

Same year, Ruth Law was the first woman to fly loop-the-loop or *loop-de-loop which is* an aerobatic maneuver where an aircraft completes a vertical *loop, making her our first female aerobatic aviator.* "Early Birds" were pilots who soloed before December 17, 1916. The organization was started in 1928 and accepted a membership of 598 pioneering aviators. Membership was limited to those who piloted a glider, gas balloon, or airplane. Women accepted into this exclusive group were: Clara Adams, Tiny Broadwick, Alys McKey Bryant, Jeanette Doty Caldwell, Helen Hodge Harris, Jean Marie Landrey, Ruth Bancroft Law, Bernetta Miller, Matilde Josephine Moisant, Lucille Belmont Rutshaw, Blanche Stuart Scott, Dorothy Rice Sims, Katherine Stinson, and her sister, Marjorie.

In 1922, the Caterpillar Club was founded by Switlik Parachute Company of Trenton, New Jersey and several other parachute manufacturers. This is an informal association of people who have successfully used a parachute to bail out of a disabled aircraft. The caterpillar references to the silk threads used in the original parachutes. On July 4, 1925, Irene McFarland, a stunt jumper, according to several sources is listed as the first female Caterpillar Club member. McFarland was to test a parachute she designed in a 3,500 foot jump. Government regulators made her wear an emergency chute. She used it when her original failed. She was accepted as a Caterpillar Club member because she did not intend to use the emergency chute which saved her life. However, many aviation historians feel Ninety-Nines charter member, Faye Gillis Wells, should be considered the first. In September, 1929, the biplane she was piloting during an aerobatic flight broke apart forcing Faye to pull her ripcord and parachute safely to the ground. Faye Gillis Wells was such a remarkable woman with so many accomplishments. She blazed trails in journalism, broadcasting and aviation.

Fabulous Firsts:

Here are a few more trailblazing women not already noted earlier for their stellar achievements.

Brown, Willa
In 1937, our first African American woman to earn a commercial flight license. As a flight instructor for more than 200 students, Brown help build the foundation for the World War II Tuskegee Airmen.

Mahlock, Lorna
In 2018, our first Black woman to achieve Brigadier General in the Marine Corps. In 1985, she enlisted. She became an Air Traffic Controller, after her 1991 officer commissioning. BZ-Bravo Zulu (Well Done) General Mahlock.

Riddle, Mary
In 1930, Riddle became the first Native American woman to earn a pilot's license. Soon after, she earned her commercial ticket. Joining an all-women barnstorming group, Mary wore traditional Native American attire as they crossed our nation in their flying show. On June 1934, May Riddle's photo appeared on the cover of the *99er*, the Ninety-Nines first magazine published for and by women pilots.

Whirly Girls (Women Helicopter Pilots) Firsts:

Rosemary Arnold
Already a fixed wing pilot in Australia, Rosemary switched to Rotary Wing. In 1965, in just four weeks, Rosemary became Australia's first. By 1967, she had attained commercial in both fixed and rotary wing. But, wait there is more. A career of firsts and fun. Rosemary is also Australia's first woman to own a helicopter charter company and be its Chief Pilot. She also founded the Helicopter Association of Australia. In 1985, Rosemary Arnold moved to Las Vegas and started a U.S. Air Charter Company.

Jacqueline Auriol
From France, Jacqueline Auriol was the first to qualify in both helicopters and jets. In 1950, Lawrence Bell invited her to take the Bell

helicopter training course. By the 1960s, Auriol set records in jet aircraft.

Ann Shaw Carter

America's first female helicopter pilot and first women commercial helicopter in the world (1947). As a former WASP, Ann earned her ratings. She was hired by Metropolitan Aviation Corporation to provide helicopter passenger services and sight-seeing in New York City. In the 1950s, polio grounded her. She continued to contribute community service and raise a family in Connecticut until her death in 2005.

Joellen Drag Oslund

In 1974, she joined five women naval aviators, Barbara Allen (Rainey), Judith Neuffer, Jane Skiles, Ana Marie Scott, and Rosemary Merims, earning Naval Wings of Gold. Joellen became the Navy's first female helicopter pilot. The entire class was inducted in the WAI Pioneer Hall of Fame.

Jean Ross Howard Phelan

In 1955, she founded the Whirly Girls. In 1941, she became a licensed pilot. By 1945, she began a storied career at the Aircraft Industries Association. In 1954, she persuaded her boss to allow her to complete the Bell Helicopter training program, making her America's 8th helicopter-rated woman pilot and 13th in the world. Upon her 1986 retirement, she had become director of helicopter activities for the now Aerospace Industries Association.

Nancy Miller Livingston Stafford

In 1947, Nancy became our first female helicopter pilot on the west coast and, later, in Juneau Alaska. She is the fourth woman in the world to earn this important rating. In 1935, Nancy was hooked on flying with her first plane ride. When World War II broke out in Europe. American volunteers joined in the fight "over the pond!" In1942, at age 23 Nancy Jane Miller joined the British Air Transport Auxiliary of the Royal Air Force. Women pilots ferried military aircraft from British factories to front-line squadrons. Nancy flew over fifty types during the war, her favorite the Spitfire. In 1970, by the end of her aviation career, Nancy flew over 100 different models.

Where did the saying **"walking on cloud nine"** come from when you are euphoric? This comes from actual cloud science. Cloud nine means we are "on top of the world" which comes from the National Weather Service, formerly U.S. Weather Bureau, numerical classification of cloud heights with nine being the highest. These are the white, puffy, billowy clouds associated with the tops of cumulonimbus clouds. The weather abbreviation is Cb. Level nine clouds can reach as high as 70,000 feet. They can appear to grow quickly as you watch them because Cumulonimbus clouds hold lots of energy with lightening, heavy showers, and strong wind gusts associated with then. They can appear to be large mountains of thick white clouds.

Where **"Balls to the Wall"** originated in aviation which means "going all out." Some military planes had throttle levers with round, ball-like tops. Pushing the throttle to the firewall meant making the aircraft fly as quickly as possible which was shortened to "Balls to the Wall."

The **Order of Daedalians** consists of American military pilots. The namesake is Daedalus, who according to Greek mythology, was the first person to achieve heavier-than-air flight.

The **OX5 Aviation Pioneers** club was organized in June, 1955 in Latrobe, Pa for the purposes of honoring aviation pioneers associated with the OX5 Engine and educating the public on matters of aeronautics. This group continues to preserve early aviation history with open membership to those interested in this mission.

Zonta International is a women's business organization similar to Rotary and Lions Clubs. In 1938, the Zontian Amelia Earhart Fellowship was established. Awarded annually to a woman pursuing a doctoral degree in aerospace-related sciences-engineering.

Mercury 13 backstory: In 1958, NASA asked for applications for their astronaut program. However, in addition to a college degree, future astronauts needed to be not only rated aviators, but military jet test pilots. As women were excluded from those military positions, the Mercury 7 were all male with "the right stuff." Privately funded by the world-famous aviator, Jackie Cochran, the Lovelace Clinic started a testing program by invitation only to experienced women in aviation to participate in similar astronaut-type testing. Stellar women committed themselves to this important research. They were:

Myrtle Cagle- a pilot with 4,300 flight time and was a mechanic age 36.

Twins Jan and Marion Dietrich. At age 35, Jan had 8,000 flying hours as a pilot for a large company. Twin Marion as an aviation journalist/pilot had 1,500 hours.

Wally Funk was the youngest at age 23. She already was a flight instructor with 3,000 hours.

Sarah Gorelick (Ratley) was an engineer and pilot with 1,800 hours and 28 years old.

Jean Hixson was 38, a school teacher, Air Force Reserve Captain and a 4,500 hour pilot.

Rhea Hurrle (Woltman), at age 31, worked as an executive pilot with 1,500 hours

Irene Leverton, also an executive pilot, had accrued 9,000 hours at age 35.

Jerri Sloan (Truhill), age 31 owned an aviation company. She had 1,200 hours.

Bea Steadman owned and operated an aviation service company. She had 8,000 hours at age 36.

Gene Nora Stumbough (Jessen) was only 25 years old with 1,450 hours as a professional pilot for an aircraft company.

All 13 women successfully underwent the very same physiological tests as the NASA Mercury 7 males. This was Phase I testing. Phase II involved isolation tank and psychological evaluations. Jerrie Cobb, Rhea Hurrle, and Wally Funk completed those tests when abruptly all further Lovelace Clinic testing was cancelled. However, over time, the story leaked out.

Their fight for women in NASA as astronauts was lost on Congressional Hill. It took until 1978, for females to be announced in the Group 8 NASA astronaut class. But, just as we now honor and remember our World War II WASP, the Mercury 13 women blazed a trail for today's women in space.

(In 1995, seven of the Mercury 13 First Lady Astronaut Trainees (FLATs) stand outside Launch Pad 39B near the Space Shuttle Discovery. (L-R) Gene Nora Jessen, Wally Funk, Jerrie Cobb, Jerri Truhill, Sarah Rutley, Myrtle Cagle, and Bernice Steadman. NASA photograph.)

Girls are capable of doing everything men are capable of doing. Sometimes, they have more imagination than men.
~ Kathryn Johnson, NASA Mathematician

11
Humor

Flying is not dangerous. However, crashing is!
~ Unknown

Research indicates humor often enhances learning and knowledge retention. The Mayo Clinic Staff recently posted a *Healthy Lifestyle* newsletter on humor, "Whether you're guffawing at a sitcom on TV or quietly giggling at a newspaper cartoon, laughing does you good. Laughter is a great form of stress relief, and that's no joke." Hollywood even made a movie, *Patch Adams*, about all the health benefits of humor.

In an April 14, 2019 on-line post at www.bigthink.com, Matt Davis wrote, "It [humor] touches upon nearly every facet of life-90 percent of men and 81 percent of women report that a sense of humor is the most important quality in a partner, it's a crucial quality for leaders…" Humor can be helpful in aviation and aerospace because often the mission is the only focus and the training and work environment are so intense.

If you are a pilot, you probably have enjoyed the laughter and learning from famed aviation speaker and flight instructor, Rod Machado. Studies indicate a relaxed atmosphere with humor contributes to increased learning and better student outcomes. With that in mind, here a few humorous sayings and stories.

From T-shirts: You can always tell an aerospace engineer. But, you can't tell them much!

Just plane happy.

Pilots: Looking Down on People Since 1903!

Real Women Fix Airplanes.

Life is Better in the Sky.

Air Traffic Controller. What is YOUR Superpower?

Aviation Dispatcher: Because Freakin' Miracle Worker isn't an official job title.

God created aircraft mechanics so pilots can have heroes, too.

God promised male pilots that excellent and subservient female aviators would be found in all corners of the world. Then, she made the earth round. She laughed and laughed and laughed some more!

Aviation Insurance Claims report: "This crash was 'pilot error'." Pilot response: "It was aircraft design error." Insurance Claim response: "Pilot error. The pilot trusted the aircraft designer."

This story made me think of my own flight training when I actually did become "hopelessly lost" because I was relying only on the airport VOR for navigation after a long cross county flight. Unfortunately I did not read the NOTAM that the VOR would be turned off that day for maintenance. "A student pilot became lost during a solo cross –county flight. Contacting Air Traffic Control in a panic, the calm voice of the female controller, asked, 'What was your last known position?' The student reply, 'When I was number one for takeoff.'"

Here is one for Airport Tower Controllers: "Jones tower, Cessna 12345, student pilot, I am out of fuel." Tower immediate responds: "Roger Cessna 12345, reduce airspeed to best glide!! Do you have the airfield in sight?!?!!" Cessna transmits: "Uh...tower, I am on the south ramp; I just want to know where the fuel truck is"

Overheard by staff from airport manager and engineer loudly discussing an issue: "I am NOT arguing. I am just explaining why I am correct!"

The pessimist sees the glass as half-empty. The optimist says it is half-full. The Airport Consultant explains why the glass needs to be twice as big to meet current design criteria.

How many pilots does it take to screw in a light bulb? Only one because they just hold up the light bulb in their hand and the world revolves around them.

Five people were hanging on to a single rope suspended from a helicopter trying to bring them to safety. Four were men. One was a Ninety-Nine. They all decided that one person would have to let go because if they didn't, the rope would break and all of them would die.

No one could decide who it should be. Finally the 99 gave a really touching speech, saying how she would give up her life to save the others because women were used to giving for the greater good. All of the men started clapping.

The nine-year old girl was asked on a health quiz, "What is a terminal illness?" Her immediate response was "when you are sick at the airport."

Supposedly these came from South African Kulula Flight Attendants but could easily be heard on other carriers. Flight Attendant safety briefings:

"People, there may be 50 ways to leave your lover, but only four on this airplane."

"To operate your seat belt just insert the metal tab into the buckle and pull tight. It works just like every other seat belt. If you don't know how to operate one, maybe you should not be travelling unsupervised."

"In the event of a sudden loss of cabin pressure, masks will automatically descend from the ceiling. Please stop screaming. Grab the mask, and pull it over your face. If you are traveling with a child, secure your mask first before assisting with theirs. If you are traveling with more than one child, pick your favorite. If traveling with more than two, 'what were you thinking?'"

After a less than stellar landing, "Please remain seated with your seat belts securely fastened while the Captain taxis what is left of our airplane to the gate!" A few seconds later, "We ask you to please stay seated while Captain Kangaroo bounces our way to the terminal." And,

"Ladies and Gentlemen, you must remain in your seat with those seatbelts more secure than ever until Captain Crash and his crew have brought the aircraft to a screeching halt against the gate. And, once the tire smoke has cleared and the warning bells are silenced, we will immediately open the door so you can pick your way through the wreckage to the safety of the terminal."

The flight attendant asked the passenger if he wanted dinner. "What are my choices?" he said. Her reply, "Yes or No!"

12
Sky and Space Success Secrets

Understanding how things work and being an engineer led me to become a helicopter pilot and eventually to NASA. The path doesn't necessarily have to be straight, but don't limit yourself to what you know. Go out and try new things.
~ Sunita Williams, Record-Setting NASA Astronaut.

Women can learn important life and career success lessons from reading and listening to the stories of other females in our career field. All these stories, words, and advice shared provide several lessons for success in aviation and aerospace.

1. There is no ONE thing.

You are the one who has to design your own flight plan.

Just as in the legend of the Gordian knot, which is really just a metaphor for problem solving, find an approach which is just a different solution to the perceived constraints or road blocks. Remember, you can go around, over, under, through, or even blow the road block up to clear your way.

2. Know yourself.

Try different things to build your confidence and comfort levels. Explore on-line, free career aptitude assessment tools. You Tube career videos, books, career fairs, internships, or just hang out at aviation businesses and airports are all excellent ways to help you on your journey of exploration.

3. Feed your mind with stories of successful women.

Books and videos are easily available. The next chapter includes ideas for you to "Explore More." Here are just a few examples of Aviation and Space Women films which can be relaxing and inspiring.

As early as 1920, 18 year old, Phoebe Fairgrave, later Omlie, determined she would become an aviation stuntwoman in the movies. By 1921, she had already set a world women's parachute drop record of over 15,000 feet. Fox Moving Picture Company hired Phoebe to wing walk in their *The Perils of Pauline* series. By 1927, she earned the first transport pilots license and became the first licensed female airplane mechanic. During this same period, an aerial performer under the name, "Ethel Dare," perfected walking from one airplane to another, becoming the first stunt woman to thrill assembled crowds.

Not to be left out is Gladys Ingle. In 1924, at age 26, she was accepted into the exclusive Hollywood aerial daredevil stunt group, The 13 Black Cats. She wing walked blindfolded on a Curtis JN-4 biplane over Los Angeles. She even performed archery stunts in the air perched on the planes. All of this with NO parachute, until a new 1927 law required parachutes be worn. By 1927, Hollywood was moving away from silent films to color and talkies.

In the early 1930s, many stunt pilots wanted to establish some safety guidelines for the industry and get paid for all the danger and injuries. In September 1931, several pilots met at Pancho Barnes place. Barnes was also a Hollywood's female stunt flier. By 1932, the Associated Motion Picture Pilots (AMPP) was formed. Working with a wage scale based on the 13 Black Cats' fees, the AMPP took control of the industry's aviation stunt work.

Years later, in 1988, daredevil, Florence Pancho Barnes, was portrayed in a television movie starring Valerie Bertinelli. In 1994, Diane Keaton played Amelia Earhart in the made-for-TV movie, *The Final Flight*. The mystery of Earhart's disappearance continues to fascinate.

In 2009, Hilary Swank as Amelia pops to mind. I love the backstory of the plane which "starred" for most of the film. Joe Shepherd of Fayetteville, GA restored his Lockheed Electra 12A Junior lovingly for 18 years when he was contacted by the producers. They needed his plane pronto because they could not find a Lockheed 10 in time for production. Shepherd found himself sweating in the cockpit of his just restored plane on a very hot summer day, having his mustache shaved off, make-up on, wearing a wig and scarf to make him look from a distance like Amelia Earhart or Hilary Swank playing Amelia. Although artistic license with some facts of history, this movie is popcorn fun.

As more backstory, Hilary took her role so seriously she already had 19 hours of flying experience before the movie's premiere. According to October 21, 2009, "Access Hollywood," Swank said, "You have to fly solo, obviously, to get your pilot's license and the insurance policy on the movie was never going to allow me to do that." The Oscar-winning star told the *Chicago Sun-Times* that "Amelia's life was certainly short. But, she accomplished so much in her lifetime. She was also a reminder to me that you constantly have to look within. You have to also live for yourself and not other people."

The Black women scientists of NASA met the challenge of outer space. The 2016, *Hidden Figures* biographical drama of how they helped send America successfully into space was highly-acclaimed, earning three Academy Award nominations. The lives of space engineer, Mary Jackson, mathematician, Katherine Johnson, and their NASA supervisor, Dorothy Vaughan, revealed the often hidden history of the many and significant contributions of women and untold 'her stories."

Significant documentary films as award-winning Heather Taylor's *Breaking through the Clouds* about the 1929 Air Derby, and the more recent *Fly Like A Girl* by Katie McEntire Wiatt are easy viewing with no tissues needed. *She Wore Silver Wings*, the true story of WWII ferrying pilot, Jean Landis, and the earlier *American Experience Fly Girls* 1999 episode are true stories. In 2015, another award-winning Bill Suchy video documentary, *Silver Wings, Flying Dreams: The Complete Story of the Women Airforce Service Pilots* starred real WASP Bee Falk Haydu and Shirley Chase Kruse.

In 2012, another documentary, *Pearl Carter Scott: On Top of the World*, and the earlier award-winning *Pearl The Movie-Pearl Carter Scott, the Youngest Pilot in History*, tell the incredible story of Oklahoma aviation legend and Chickasaw native, Eula "Pearl" Carter Scott, taught how to fly by Wiley Post. On September 12, 1929, Pearl flew solo at age 13, making her the youngest Native American female pilot. Popular "entertainment" should be used more often to share some of the amazing stories of our women in air and space history.

As early as the 1966, popular television show, "Star Trek," Black actress, Nichelle Nichols, portrayed Lt. Nyota Uhura, on the bridge of the USS Starship Enterprise as the important crew communications officer. She showed young women what they could do. Interesting *Nyota* is the Swahili word for "star." Even today's more recent *Star Wars* releases depict women as aerial fighters and strong leaders.

The 1996, the gripping Meg Ryan film, *Courage Under Fire*, about a female Black Hawk medivac chopper pilot, killed in action, being considered as the first woman to receive the Medal of Honor, posthumously. Spoiler alert: Her orphaned daughter receives her Medal of Honor in the formal ceremony at the end of the movie. Tissues in order for this inspiring work of fiction.

Inspiring films, docudramas, and documentaries about women in sky and space exist in almost any language. A 2018, film titled, *A Mirror for the Sun*, is about combat navigator, Tamar Ariel, who became the first woman Orthodox Jew to train in that role in the Israeli Defense Force.

Inspiring cinema can feed your mind as you munch on that hot-buttered popcorn. Just as aviation and aerospace is awesome to experience, film, books, and music can transport you to a "happy place." You decide how to feed your mind each day.

4. Write a plan with short and longer term steps you can work on daily.

See yourself achieving those goals by staging photographs so that you constantly "see" your success. In your personal plan include possible sources for personal and financial support for success.

5. Commit to doing the difficult.

Reward yourself with special private and public celebrations along the way for the successful steps.

6. Create personal support groups to help you mark those important career milestones.

The Explore More chapter lists organizations and associations to encourage you in aviation and aerospace careers.

7. Reach out to industry professionals through joining their associations and visiting their web sites often to learn about new opportunities, training and technology

8. This is a long journey and you need a good ground crew to help you focus.

I am not the original author of this story which has several variations and names. But, it serves a good purpose to help you reflect on the many life lessons and experiences shared throughout this book.

The Jar of Life

When things in your life seem almost too much to handle, when 24 hours in a day are not enough, remember this story.

A professor stood before her philosophy class and had some items in front of her on a table. When the class began, she wordlessly picked up a very large and empty mayonnaise jar and proceeded to fill it with golf balls. She then asked the students if the jar was full. They agreed that it was.

The professor then picked up a box of tiny pebbles and poured them into the jar. She shook the jar lightly. The pebbles rolled into the open areas between the golf balls. She then asked the students again if the jar was full. They still agreed it was.

The professor next picked up a box of sand and poured it into the jar. Of course, the sand filled up everything else. She asked once more if the jar was full. The students responded unanimously, "YES!"

The professor then produced a glass of wine from under the table and poured the entire contents into the jar effectively filling the empty space between the sand. The students laughed.

"Now," said the professor as the laughter subsided, "I want you to recognize that this jar represents your life. The golf balls are the important things---your family, your children, your health, your pets, your friends, and your favorite passions---and if everything else was lost and only they remained, your life would still be full.

"The pebbles are the other things that matter like your job, house, airplane, and car.

"The sand is everything else---the small stuff. If you put the sand into the jar first, there is no room for the pebbles or the golf balls. The same goes for life. If you spend all your time and energy on the small stuff, you will never have room for the things that are important to you.

"Pay attention to the things that are critical to your happiness. Focus on the big things. Take care of the golf balls first---the things that really matter. Set your priorities. The rest is just sand or small stuff."

One of the students raised her hand and inquired what the wine represented. The professor smiled and said, "I'm glad you asked. The wine just shows you that no matter how full your life may seem, there is always room for a glass of wine shared with a friend or family."

9. Lastly, YOU reach out to young girls and women with a sincere offer to listen and share.

10. My personal message to you.

Always remember helping one person may not change the whole world. But, it WILL change one person's world forever. I believe that often the mountains which seem to block our way to our goal are only seen by us and the mountain is either imagined or made larger in our mind. These words and stories from the Sky Stars in this book show the way to "roar and soar." I encourage you to climb your own mountains. Once you reach your mountain top, breathe deeply, and savor the view. Then, look for a bigger mountain!

And, remember to enjoy this moment because it is God's gift to us. That is why we call it, the present.

EPILOGUE
Celebrating The Life of
Captain Emily Howell Warner

By Donna Miller, reprinted with permission, July-August
2020 Ninety-Nines magazine

"Good Morning, Ladies and Gentlemen, from the flight deck, this is your Captain speaking." It is because of Emily Howell Warner that it is possible to hear those words spoken by a woman. And today, as we pilots watch her quietly bank her aircraft, and roll out onto a heading of 270 to "head west" (by instruction of the Ultimate Air Traffic Controller), we celebrate her life here on earth.

It is because of Emily that little girls, seeing a woman pilot as she boards the plane, can picture the career of an airline pilot as a viable option. But Emily had no pilot role models. In fact, as she began to dream her dreams of an airline career, she had more people telling her that it couldn't be done than she had encouraging her.

Imagine being a flight instructor with thousands of flight hours, teaching young men to fly. Under Emily's guidance, many of these men went on to be successful airline pilots. But that wasn't an option for Emily. How hard it must have been for Emily to live in her propeller driven world, and look through the glass ceiling at the jets flying high above, knowing THAT's where she wanted to be. And so her quest began.

It is said that success is where being prepared meets opportunity. Emily was more than prepared, and through creative staging, with the help of a few allies, she created the opportunity that would allow her to live her passion and eventually become the first woman airline Captain in the United States.

It was with grace and equanimity that Emily navigated an often harsh environment at the airline. Knowing the gauntlet she ran each time she went to work, we can get a glimpse of the depth of her passion for flying. There were many men who didn't want a girl in their good old boys club, no matter how qualified she was It was a great day when, to show their acceptance of her, one of the tougher captains said to her, "Emily, you're just one of the fellas now." Emily always beamed with twinkling eyes when she told us that story. To show how far Emily has taken us, I flew with a Captain recently, and after he made a particularly nice landing, I said, "Mike, you fly like a girl!" And he said, "Thank you."

Emily has motivated prospective pilots and young girls through inspiring talks. While telling us HOW she became an airline pilot, she showed us that it's possible to be strong without being hard, and that we could be smart without being intimidating. I have seen Emily surrounded by girl scouts who were mesmerized by her stories of flying and without realizing it, they could see the possibilities for their own lives.

At the Smithsonian Air and Space museum in Washington D.C. Captain Warner's uniform is on display. Frankly, if they hang your laundry at the Smithsonian, you know you have arrived. And today as we say goodbye to Emily, it's safe to say she has arrived in Heaven, having greased the landing of her jet with a woman's touch, right on schedule. If you're thinking of Emily and see a rainbow or a butterfly or an Irish four-leaf clover, it's probably her because Heaven's Tower has asked her to contact ground.

(2014 NAHF acceptance Emily Howell Warner. Penny Hamilton photographer.)

Donna Miller flies the 787 Dreamliner for a major airline. Her aviation career began in South Korea where she earned her private pilot license while working as a civilian for the U.S. Air Force. Her aviation experience includes flying cargo, skydivers, passengers, professional sports teams, air ambulance, and charter flights worldwide. She is a featured writer in the national publications of the International Ninety-Nines and Women in Aviation International.

You can be great. You can rattle the stars. You can do anything, if only you dare and persist. ~ Unknown

EXPLORE MORE

BOOKS

Albion, Michele Wehrwein, editor. *The Quotable Amelia Earhart*. Albuquerque, NM: University of New Mexico Press, 2015.

Anderson, Nancy P. *The Very Few, The Proud Women in the Marine Corps, 1977-2001*. Quantico, VA: History Division United States Marine Corps, 2018.

Angell, Janet. *Jump Seat: 1963-1976 A Stewardess Memoir*. Seattle WA: CreateSpace, 2017.

Annis, Barbara and John Gray. *Work With Me: The 8 Blind Spots Between Men and Women in Business*. New York: St. Martin's Press, 2013.

Aragon, Cecilia. *Flying Free: My Victory over Fear to Become the First Latina Pilot on the US Aerobatic Team*. Ashland OR: Blackstone Publishing, 2020.

Armour, Vernice "FlyGirl," foreword by Mae Jemison, M.D. *Zero to Breakthrough: The 7-Step, Battle-Tested Method for Accomplishing Goals That Matter*. New York: Avery Publishing, 2011.

Atkins, Jeannine. *Wings and Rockets: The Story of Women in Air and Space*. New York: Farrar, Straus, and Giroux, 2003.

Auriol, Jacqueline. *I Live to Fly*. Boston: E.P. Dutton, 1970.

Baldwin, James Patrick "Jamie" and Jeff Kriendler. *Pan American World Airways Aviation History through the Words of its People*. Saint Augustine, FL: Bluewater Press, LLC, 2011.

Banglesdorf, Rene and Lisa Copeland. *Crushing Mediocrity: 10 Ways to Rise Above the Status Quo*. Georgetown TX: Crushing It Academy, LLC, 2016.

Bass, Beverley with Cynthia Williams and pictures by Joanie Stone. *Me and the Sky: Captain Beverley Bass, Pioneering Pilot.* New York: Alfred A. Knopf, 2019.

Beaton, Gail M. *Colorado Women in World War II.* Louisville, CO: University Press of Colorado, 2020.

Bell-Pearson, Edna. *Headwinds: A Memoir by Edna Bell-Pearson.* Emporia, KS. Meadowlark Books, 2020.

Benge, Janet and Geoff Benge. *Betty Greene: Wings to Serve* Seattle: WA: YWAM Publishing, 1991.

Bergman, Ziva. *Aviation Humor.* The Netherlands: Martin Leeuwis Publication, 2012.

Bjorkman, Eileen A. *The Propeller Under the Bed: A Personal History of Homebuilt Aircraft.* Seattle WA: University of Washington Press, 2019.

Bosca, Caro Bayley. *Women Airforce Service Pilots, Class of 43-W-7: Letters 1943-44.* Denton TX: Texas Woman's University Special Collections, 1995.

Bower, Jennifer Bean, foreword by Cris Takacs. *North Carolina Aviatrix Viola Gentry: The Flying Cashier.* Charleston, SC: The History Press, 2015.

Bragg, Janet Harmon as told to Marjorie M. Kriz. *Soaring Above Setbacks: The Autobiography of Janet Harmon Bragg.* Washington, DC: Smithsonian Institute Press, 1997.

Bridges, Donna, Jane Neal-Smith and Albert Mills, editors. *Absent Aviators: Gender Issues in Aviation.* London: Ashgate Publishing, 2014, paperback edition 2020.

Burgess, Colin, foreword by Grace George Corrigan. *Teacher in Space: Christa McAuliff and the Challenger Legacy.* Lincoln, NE: University of Nebraska Press, 2020.

Butler, Susan. *East to the Dawn: The Life of Amelia Earhart.* New York: Da Capo Press, 1999.

Cadogan, Mary. *Women with Wings: Female Flyers in Fact and Fiction.* Chicago: Chicago Academy Publishers, 1993.

Carl, Ann Baumgartner. *A WASP Among Eagles.* Washington DC: Smithsonian Institution Press, 1999.

Case, Betsy. *Trailblazers: The Women of the Boeing Company.* Ironwood Lithographics, 2014.

Cavallaro, Umberto. *Women Spacefarers: Sixty Different Paths to Space.* New York: Springer Praxis Books, 2017.

Chung, Stephanie. *Profit Like A Girl: A Woman's Guide to Kicking Butt in Sales and Leadership.* Publisher Stephanie Chung and Associates, 2016. Kindle

Clark, Julie with Ann Lewis Cooper. *Nothing Stood in Her Way: Captain Julie Clark.* West Alexandria, OH: Women in Aviation Intl., 2004.

Cobb, Jerrie. *Jerrie Cobb, Solo Pilot.* Sun City Center, FL: Jerrie Cobb Foundation, Inc., 1997.

Cobb, Jerrie and Jane Rieker. *Woman Into Space: The Jerrie Cobb Story.* Whitefish, MT: Literary Licensing LLC, 2012.

Cooper, Ann Lewis. *Weaving the Winds, Emily Howell Warner.* Bloomington, IN: 1st Books Library, 2003.

Cooper, Ann Lewis and art by Sharon Rajnus. *Stars of the Sky, Legends All: Illustrated Histories of Women Aviation Pioneers.* St. Paul, MN: Zenith Press, 2008.

Cox, Jessica. *Disarm Your Limits: The Flight Formula to Lift You to Success and Propel You to the Next Horizon.* Rightfooted Publishing: Tucson AZ, 2005.

Culea, John and contributors Patti Culea, George Gewehr, and Janet Burttram. *One-way or Round Trip: Women Flight Attendants and Troops During the Vietnam War.* Lufkin, TX: Independently published, 2019.

Cummins, Julie with illustrations by Marlene R. Laugesen. *Flying Solo: How Ruth Elder Soared into America's Heart.* New York: Roaring Brook Press, 2013.

Cummins, Julie. *Tomboy of the Air: Daredevil Pilot Blanche Stuart Scott.* HarperCollins Publishers LLC: New York, 2001.

Diehn, Andi and Katie Mazeika illustrator. *Space Adventurer: Bonnie Dunbar, Astronaut*. White River Junction VT: Nomad Press, 2019.

Donnelly, Karen J. *American Women Pilots of World War II*. New York: Rosen Publishing Group, 2004.

Erisman, Fred. *In Their Own Words: Forgotten Women Pilots of Early Aviation*. West Lafayette IN: Purdue University Press, 2021.

Farney, Dennis. *The Barnstormer and the Lady: Walter and Olive Ann Beech*. Kansas City, MO: Rockhill Books, 2010.

Freni, Pamela. *Space for Women: A History of Women with the Right Stuff*. Santa Ana, CA: Seven Locks Press, 2002.

Frosell da Ponte, Heddy. *The Glamour Years of Flying as a Stewardess* (Memoir). Publisher Heddy Frosell da Ponte, 2019.

Garratt, CarolAnn. *Upon Silver Wings: Global Adventures in a Small Plane*. Garratt Publisher, 2004.

---. *Upon Silver Wings II: World Record Adventures*. Garratt Publisher, 2009.

---.*Upon Silver Wings III: People and Places Around the World*. Garratt Publisher, 2012.

Garstecki, Julia. *WASPS*. North Mankato MN: Black Rabbit Books, 2017.

Gibson, Karen Bush. *Women Aviators: 26 Stories of Pioneer Flights, Daring Missions, and Record-Setting Journeys*. Chicago: Chicago Review Press, 2013.

---. *Women in Space: 23 Stories of First Flights, Scientific Missions, and Gravity-Breaking Adventures*. Chicago: Chicago Review Press, 2020.

Gosnell, Mariana. *Zero 3 Bravo: Solo Across America in a Small Plane*. New York: Knopf, 1993.

Hale, Julian. *Women in Aviation*. London: Shire Publications, 2019.

Hall, Ed. Y. *Harriet Quimby: America's First Lady of the Air*. Spartanburg, SC: Honoribus Press, 1990.

Hall, Loretta. *Space Pioneers in their own words*. Rio Grande Books and LPD Press, 2014.

Hamilton, Penny Rafferty. *America's Amazing Airports: Connecting Communities to the World!* Granby, CO: Mountaintop Legacy Press, 2019.

Harris, Grace McAdams. *West to Sunrise.* Ames IA: Iowa State University Press, 1980.

Harrison, Jean-Pierre. *The Edge of Time: The Authoritative Biography of Kalpana Chawla.* Los Gatos, CA: Harrison Publishing, 2011.

Haydu, Bernice "Bee" Falk. *Letters Home 1944-1945: Women Airforce Service Pilots.* Jupiter, FL: TopLine Printing and Graphics, 2003.

Hegar, Mary Jennings. *Shoot like a Girl: One woman's dramatic fight in Afghanistan and on the home front.* New York: Berkley, 2018.

Hirschman, Loree Draude and Dave Hirschman. *She's Just Another Navy Pilot: An Aviator's Sea Journal.* Newport RI: U.S. Naval Institute Press, 2000.

Hodgman, Ann, and Rudy Djabbaroff. *Sky Stars: the History of Women in Aviation.* New York, NY: Atheneum, 1981.

Hodgson, Marion Stegeman. *Winning My Wings: A Woman Airforce Service Pilot in World War II.* Annapolis, MD: Naval Institute Press, 1996.

Holden, Henry M. *Hovering: The History of the Whirly-Girls: International Women Helicopter Pilots.* Freedom NJ: Blackhawk Publishing Company, 1994.

Holmstedt, Kirsten, foreword by Maj. L. Tammy Duckworth. *Band of Sisters: American Women at War in Iraq.* Mechanicsburg, PA: Stackpole Books, 2007.

Holt, Nathalia. *Rise of the Rocket Girls: The Women Who Propelled Us, from Missiles to the Moon to Mars.* Boston: Little, Brown & Co., 2016.

Jackson, Libby. *Galaxy Girls: 50 Amazing Stories of Women in Space.* New York: Harper Design, 2018.

James, Deborah Lee, foreword by Sheryl Sandberg. *Aim High: Chart Your Course and Find Success.* New York: Post Hill Press, 2019.

Jemison, Mae. *Find Where the Wind Goes: Moments From My Life.* New York: Scholastic Press, 2001.

Jessen, Gene Nora. *The Fabulous Flight of The Three Musketeers: A Rollicking Airplane Adventure With A Few Thrills*. Charleston, SC: BookSurge Publishing, 2009.

Jessen, Gene Nora, foreword by Eileen Collins. *Sky Girls: The True Story of the First Women's Cross-Country Air Race*. Naperville, IL: Sourcebooks, 2018.

Johnson, Caroline with Hof Williams. *Jet Girl: My Life in War, Peace, and the Cockpit of the Navy's Most Lethal Aircraft, the F/A-18 Super Hornet*. New York: St. Martin's Press, 2019.

Johnson, Katherine. *Reaching for the Moon: The Autobiography of NASA Mathematician Katherine Johnson*. New York: Atheneur Books for Young Readers, 2020.

Kahn, Karen M. *Flight Guide to Success: Tips and Tactics for the Aspiring Airline Pilot*: Santa Barbara, CA: Cheltenham, 1997, current 3rd edition 2003.

Kardon, Robin R.D. *FLYGIRL* (novel). Irvine CA: Acorn Publishing, 2018.

Keil, Sally Van Wagenen. *Those Wonder Women in Their Flying Machines: The Unknown Heroines of World War II*. New York: Rawson, Wade publishers, Inc., 1979. (Updated and reprinted 1990)

Kerr, Anne Billingsley. *Fujiyama Trays & Oshibori Towels Recalling A Time When Passenger Flight was an Adventure and the Boeing Strato-cruiser ruled the skies*. Minneapolis MN: Lady Skywriter Publications, 2009 and 2nd Ed 2015.

Kinsella, Mary E. editor. *Women in Aerospace Materials: Advancements and Perspectives of Emerging Technologies*. Cham Switzerland, Springer Publishing, 2020.

Klepeis, Alicia Z. and Hui Li illustrator. *Gutsy Girls Go For Science: Astronauts: With Stem Projects for Kids*. White River Junction VT: Nomad Press, 2019.

Laidlaw, Linda. *Coffee, Tea and Rock 'N' Roll: Memoirs of a Stewardess Flying the World's Greatest Bands*. La Rocca Publishing, 2016.

Lambert, Paul F. *Never Give Up! The Life of Pearl Carter Scott*. Ada OK: The Chickasaw Press, 2009.

Landdeck, Katherine Sharp. *The Women with Silver Wings: The Inspiring True Story of the Women Airforce Service Pilots of World War II*. New York: Crown, 2020.

Lang, Heather and Raul Colon illustrator. *Fearless Flyer: Ruth Law and Her Flying Machine*. Westminister, MD: Calkins Creek, 2016.

Langley, Wanda. *Flying Higher: The Women Airforce Service Pilots of World War II*. Linnet Books, 2002.

Larson, Kirsten W. and Tracy Subisak illustrator. *Wood, Wire, Wings: Emma Lilian Todd Invents an Airplane*. Toronto: Calkins Creek, 2020.

Lear, Moya. *Bill and Moya Lear, An Unforgettable Flight*. Publisher Jack Bacon, 1996.

Lebow, Eileen F. *Before Amelia: Women Pilots in the Early Days of Aviation*. Washington, DC: Brassey's Inc., 2002.

Lenthe, Jean-Vi. *Flying Into Yesterday: My Search for the Curtiss-Wright Aeronautical Engineering Cadettes*. El Prado, NM: Wild Hare Press, 2011.

Leppert, Ashlee. *The Hurricane Within*. Mandi Pants Press, LLC, 2019.

Lovell, Mary S. *Straight On Till Morning: the Biography of Beryl Markham*. New York: St. Martin's Press, 1987.

Lunken, Martha and Mac McClellan. *Unusual Attitudes: Obsessions and Confessions of a Lady Pilot*. Batavia, OH: Sporty's Pilot Shop, 2016.

Maloney, Linda (editor). *Military Fly Moms: Sharing Memories, Building Legacies, Inspiring Hope*. Tannenbaum Publishing Co, 2012.

Markhan, Beryl. *West with the Night*. Boston, MA: Houghton Mifflin Company, 1942.

McAllister, Bruce and Stephan Wilkinson. *Skygirls: A Photographic History of the Airline Stewardess*. Roundup Press, 2012.

McCarthy, Meghan. *Daredevil: The Daring Life of Betty Skelton*. Holland OH: Dreamscape Media, 2013.

McLaren, Teri and Bobby Garcia. *The W.A.S.P. Sisters of the Sky* (novel). Sebring, FL: Saphirion Press, Inc., 2016.

McSally, Martha. *Dare to Fly: Simple Lessons in Never Giving Up.* New York: William Morrow & Company, 2020.

Meloche, Renee Taft and illustrator, Bryan Pollard. *Betty Greene: Flying High* (Heroes for Young Readers series). Seattle WA: YWAM Publishing, 2004.

Merry, Lois K. *Women Military Pilots of World War II: A History with Biographies of American, British, Russian, and German Aviators.* Jefferson, NC: McFarland & Co., 2011.

Merryman, Molly. *Clipped Wings: The Rise and Fall of the Women Airforce Service Pilots (WASPs) of World War II.* New York: New York University Press, 1998.

Miller, Erin. *Final Flight Final Fight: My grandmother, the WASP, and Arlington National Cemetery.* 4336 Press, LLC, 2019.

Miller, William M. *To Live and Die a WASP: 38 Women Pilots Who Died in WWII*, Seattle WA: CreateSpace Independent Publishing Platform, 2016.

Mitchell, Charles R. and Kirk W. House. *Flying High: Pioneer Women in American Aviation.* Charleston, SC: Arcadia Publishing, 2002.

Muir, Elizabeth Gillan. *Canadian Women in the Sky: 100 Years of Flight.* Toronto Canada: Dundurn Group, 2015.

Mundy, Liza. *Code Girls: The Untold Story of the American Women Code Breakers of World War II.* New York, NY: Hachette Books, 2017.

Myles, Bruce. *Night Witches: The Amazing Story of Russia's Women Pilots in World War II.* Chicago: Academy Chicago Publishers, 1997 edition.

Nathan, Amy, foreword by NASA Astronaut Eileen Collings. *Yankee Doodle Gals: Women Pilots of World War II.* Washington, DC: National Geographic Society, 2001.

Nelson, Sue. *Wally Funk's Race For Space: The Extraordinary Story of a Female Pioneer.* Chicago: Chicago Review Press, 2019.

Nesch, Sonya. *WWII, Betrayal, Then Congressional Gold Medal: A Great Ride for WASP Jean Landis.* London: Trillium Press, 2019.

Nichols, Ruth, foreword by Richard E. Byrd, Dorothy Roe Lewis editor. *Wings for Life: The Life Story of the First Lady of the Air.* Philadelphia: J.D. Lippincott, 1957.

Noggle, Anne, introduction by Christine A. White. *A Dance with Death: Soviet Airwomen in World War II World's First Women Combat Fliers!* College Station, TX: Texas A & M University Press, 2001.

Nolen, Stephanie. *Promised The Moon: The Untold Story of the first Women in the Space Race.* New York: Thunder's Mouth Press, 2004.

O'Brien, Keith. *Fly Girls: How Five Daring Women Defied All Odds and Made Aviation History.* Boston, MA: Houghton Mifflin Harcourt, 2019.

O'Neill, Nora. *Flying Tigress: A Memoir.* Seattle, WA: Ascending Journey Press, 2005.

O'Shaughnessy, Tam. *Sally Ride: A Photobiography of America's Pioneering Woman in Space.* New York: Roaring Brook Press, 2017.

Owens, Lisa L. *Women Pilots of World War II.* Minneapolis, MN: Lerner Publishing Group, 2019.

Parrish, Nancy Allyson. *WASP: In Their Own Words: An Illustrated History.* Wings Across America Publications, 2010.

Pearson, Patricia O'Connell. *Fly Girls: The Daring American Women Pilots Who Helped Win WWII.* New York: Simon & Schuster Books for Young Readers, Reprint edition 2019.

Pellegreno, Ann Holtgreen. *World Flight: The Earhart Trail.* Ames, IO: Iowa State University Press, 1971.

Petitt, Karlene. *Flight to Success: Be The Captian of Your Life.* Seattle, WA: Jet Star Publishing, 2015.

Petrick, Neila Skinner, illustrated by Daggi Wallace. *Katherine Stinson Otero: High Flyer.* New Orleans, LA: Pelican Publishing Company, 2006.

Pimm, Nancy Roe and illustrator Alexandra Bye. *Fly, Girl, Fly! Shaesta Waiz Soars the World.* Minneapolis MN: Beaming Books, 2020.

Pimm, Nancy Roe. *The Jerrie Mock Story: The First Woman to Fly Solo Around the World.* Athens OH: Ohio University Press, 2016.

Polson, Shannon Huffman. *The Grit Factor: Courage, Resilience, and Leadership in the Most Male-Dominated Organization in the World.* Boston: Harvard Business Review Press, 2020.

Render, Shirley, foreword by Punch Dickins. *No Place For A Lady! The Story of Canadian Women Pilots, 1928-1992.* Winnipeg, Manitoba: Portage & Main Press, 1992.

Rezaee, Arman. *50+ skills that make your life easier as a Flight Dispatcher + Real Interview Tips.* Independent Publisher, 2019.

Rickman, Sarah Byrn. *BJ Erickson: WASP Pilot.* Palmer Lake, CO: Filter Press, LLC, 2018.

---*The Originals: The Women's Auxiliary Ferrying Squadron of WWII.* Springboro, OH: Braughler Books LLC, 2017.

---*Finding Dorothy Scott: Letters of a WASP.* Lubbock, TX: Texas Tech University Press, 2016.

---*Nancy Love WASP Pilot.* Palmer Lake, CO: Filter Press LLC, 2019.

Rickman, Sarah Bryn with foreword by Deborah G. Douglas. *Nancy Love and the WASP Ferry Pilots of World War II.* Denton, TX: University of North Texas, 2008.

Rickman, Sarah Bryn with foreword by Trish Beckman, Commander US Navy (retired). *Flight to Destiny.* Springboro, OH: Braughler Books, LLC, 2017. (Fiction)

Rickman, Sarah Bryn with foreword by Deborah G. Douglas. *WASP of the Ferry Command: Women Pilots, Uncommon Deeds.* Denton, TX: University of North Texas Press, 2017.

Ride, Sally with Susan Okie. *To Space and Back.* New York: Lothrop, Lee & Shepard Books, 1989.

Riegel, Betty. *Up in the Air: The Real Story of Life Aboard the World's Most Glamorous Airline.* Simon & Schuster UK (2013) and Abby Publishing, revised 2020.

Ringenberg, Margaret J. *Girls Can't Be Pilots: An Aerobiography.* United Kingdom: Daedalus Press Books, 1998.

Roberson, Elizabeth Whitney. *Tiny Broadwick: The First Lady of Parachuting*. New Orleans, LA: Pelican Publishing, 2001.

Rossmark, Sharon, and Wendy Erikson, Cameron Wilson illustrator. *Drone Girls and the Air Show Adventure*. Zayos, 2018.

Russo, Carolyn. *Women and Flight: Portraits of Contemporary Women Pilots*. Washington, D.C.: National Air and Space Museum, 1997.

Ryan, Gretchen. *Secrets of a Stewardess: Flying the World in the 1980s*. Stroud UK: The History Press, 2019.

Schrader, Helen. *Sisters in Arms*. Barnsley, England: Pen & Sword Aviation, 2015.

Seddon, Rhea. *Go For Orbit: One of America's First Women Astronauts Finds Her Space.* Your Space Press, 2015.

Seemann, Kitty and Bob Seemann (authors), Ann Cooper (editor). *Wings of Her Dreams: Alaska Bush & Glacier Pilot, Kitty Banner*. London: Pogo Press, 2018.

Settles, Lauren Dalzell. *Could I be a Pilot? Evie's Journey to Becoming a Pilot*. Victoria BC (Canada): Friesen Press, 2020.

Sheinkin, Steve, illustrator Bijou Karman. *Born to Fly: The First Women's Air Race Across America*. New York: Roaring Brook Press, 2019.

Sherman, Janann. *Walking on Air: The Aerial Adventures of Phoebe Omlie*. Jackson MS: University Press of Mississippi, 2011.

Sherr, Lynn. *Sally Ride: America's First Woman in Space*. New York: Simon & Schuster, 2015.

Shetterly, Margot Lee. *Hidden Figures: The American Dream of the Black Women Mathematicians Who Helped Win the Space Race*. New York, NY: William Morrow, 2016.

Shipko, Mary Bush. *Aviatrix: First Woman Pilot for Hughes Airwest*. Seattle, WA: CreateSpace Publishing, 2015.

Shipko, Mary Bush, Kathy McCullough, Bonnie Tiburzi Caputo. *Women Who Fly: True Stories by Women Airline Pilots*. Las Vegas, NV: International Society of Women Airline Pilots, 2018.

Shults, Tammie Jo. *Nerves of Steel: How I Followed My Dreams, Earned My Wings, And Faced My Greatest Challenge.* Nashville, TN: Thomas Nelson, 2019.

Siegel, Rebecca. *To Fly Among The Stars: the Hidden Story of the Fight for Women Astronauts.* New York: Scholastic Focus, 2020.

Simons, Lisa M. Bolt. *The U.S. WASP: Trailblazing Women Pilots of World War II.* North Mankato, MN: Capstone Press, 2018.

Smith, Amber. *Danger Close: My Epic Journey as a Combat Helicopter Pilot in Iraq and Afghanistan.* New York: Atria Books, 2017.

Smith-Daugherty, Rhonda. *Jacqueline Cochran: Biography of a Pioneer Aviator.* Jefferson, NC: McFarland Publishing, 2012.

Sorell, Taci and Natasha Donovan illustrator. *Classified: The Secret Career of Mary Golda Ross, Cherokee Aerospace Engineer.* Minneapolis MN: Millbrook Press, 2021.

Steadman, Bernice Trimble and Josephine M. Clark. *Tethered Mercury: A Pilot's Memoir: The Right Stuff—But the Wrong Sex.* Aviation Press, 2001.

Stone, Tanya Lee. *Almost Astronauts 13 Women Who Dared to Dream.* Somerville, MA: Candlewick Press, 2009.

Stratford, Nancy Miller Livingston. *Contact! Britain! A Woman Ferry Pilot's Story During WWII in England.* Seattle WA: Createspace, 2011.

Strebe, Amy Goodpaster. *Flying For Her Country The American and Soviet Women Military Pilots of WW II.* Westport: Praeger Security International, 2007.

Sullivan, Kathryn D. *Handprints on Hubble: An Astronaut's Story of Invention.* Cambridge MA: MIT Press, 2019.

Sumner, Sandi. *Women Pilots of Alaska.* Jefferson NC: McFarland & Co., 2005

Teitel, Amy Shira. *Fighting For Space: Two Pilots and Their Historic Battle for Female Spaceflight.* New York: Grand Central Publishing, 2020.

Thaden, Louise, foreword by Patty Wagstaff. *High, Wide and Frightened.* Fayetteville AR: University of Arkansas Press, reprinted edition 2004.

Tiburzi, Bonnie. *Takeoff! The Story of America's First Woman Pilot for a Major Airline.* New York, NY: Crown Publishers, Inc., 1986.

Timofeyeva-Yegorova, Anna, Kim Green, editor, Margarita Ponomariova and Kim Green, translator. *Red Sky Black Death: A Soviet Woman Pilot's Memoir of the Eastern Front.* Bloomington IN: Slavica Publishers, 2009.

Tiscareno-Sato, Graciela, illustration by Linda Lens. *Captain Mama's Surprise/La Sorpresa de Capitan Mama.* Hayward, CA: Gracefully Global Group, LLC, 2016.

Titterington, Diane. *Speaking of Flying: Personal Tales of Heroism, Humor, Talent and Terror from 44 Unique Aviators.* San Clemente, CA: Aviation Speakers Bureau, 2000.

Turner, Lisa. *Dream Take Flight: An Unconventional Journey.* Hayesville NC: Turner Creek Publishing, 2019.

Turney, Mary Ann, editor. *Tapping Diverse Talent in Aviation: Culture, Gender, and Diversity.* Burlington, VT: Ashgate Publishing, 2004.

Vacher, Polly. *Wings Around the World: The Exhilarating Story of One Woman's Epic Flight from the North Pole to Antarctica.* London: Grub Street Publishing, 2008.

Ventura, Marne. *12 Women in the Space Industry: Women Who Changed the World.* Mankato MN: 12-Story Library, 2020.

Wagstaff, Patty with Ann L. Cooper. *Fire and Air: A Life On The Edge.* Chicago, IL: Chicago Review Press, Inc., 1997.

Walker, Diana Barnato. *Spreading My Wings.* London: Grub Street Publishing, 2008.

Wallace, Lane. *Unforgettable: My Ten Best Flights.* Batavia, OH: Sporty's Pilot Shop, 2009.

Walters, Claire L. and Betty McMillen Loufek. *This Flying Life.* Airwoman Press, 1999.

Waxman, Laura Hamilton. *Aerospace Engineer Aprille Ericsson.* Minneapolis MN: Lerner Classroom, 2015.

Weigand, Cindy. *Texas Women in World War II*. Lanham, MD: Republic of Texas Press, 2003.

Weitekamp, Margaret A. *Right Stuff, Wrong Sex: America's First Women in Space Program*. Baltimore, MD: The Johns Hopkins University Press, 2005.

Welch, Rosanne. *Encyclopedia of Women in Aviation and Space*. Santa Barbara CA: ABC-CLIO, Inc., 1998.

Williams, Vera S. *WASPs: Women Airforce Service Pilots of World War II*. London: Motorbooks International, 1994.

Winegarten, Debra L. *Katherine Stinson: the Flying Schoolgirl*. Fort Worth, TX: Eakin Press, 2000.

Wright, Marsha J. *Maggie Ray WWII Air Force Pilot*. St. Louis, MO: Pen & Publish, Inc., 2007.

Yellin, Emily. *Our Mothers War: American Women at Home and at the Front during World War II*. New York: Free Press, 2004.

York, Beth Ruggiero. *Flying Alone: A Memoir*. Beth Ruggiero York Publisher, 2019.

ONLINE RESOURCES

Able Fight www.AbleFlight.org
Aircraft Owners & Pilots Association www.aopa.org
Airport Consultants Council www.acconline.org
Air Line Pilots Association www.ALPA.org
Air Traffic Control Association www.ATCA.org
American Association of Airport Executives (AAAE) www.aaae.org
American Institute of Aeronautics and Astronautics www.AIAA.org
American Rosie the Riveter Association www.RosieTheRiveter.net
Association for Women in Aviation Maintenance www.awam.org
Association for Women in Science www.awis.org
Association of Flight Attendants-CWA www.afacwa.org
Aviation careers: jobs, salaries & educational requirements
    www.thebestschools.org/careers/aviation-careers/
Aviation Community Foundation www.aviation-community.org
Balloon Federation of America www.BFA.net
Black Pilots of America www.bpapilots.org
Drone Life www.DroneLife.com
Experimental Aircraft Association-EAA
    www.EAAWomenSoarSociety.org
Experimental Aircraft Association-EAA www.eaa.org/womenventure
Female Aviators Sticking Together-F.A.S.T. www.FASTpilots.org
Future & Active Pilot Advisors www.FAPA.aero
Future Aviation Professionals of America www.FAPA.info
Fly for the Culture www.FlyfortheCulture.org
Institute for Women of Aviation Worldwide www.iwoaw.org
International Aviation Women's Association www.iawa.org
International Society of Transport Aircraft Trading Foundation
    www.Foundation.ISTAT.org
International Society of Women Airline Pilots-ISA+21
    www.iswap.org
International Women's Air & Space Museum www.IWASM.org

Ladies Love Taildraggers www.Ladieslovetaildraggers.com
Latino Pilots Association www.LatinoPilot.org
Lighter-Than-Air Society www.blimpinfo.com
National Aeronautics and Space Administration www.NASA.gov
National Air Transportation Association www.NATA.aero
National Association of Flight Instructors www.nafinet.org
National Association of Rocketry www.NAR.org
National Association of State Aviation Officials www.nasao.org
National Business Aviation Association www.NBAA.org
National WASP WWII Museum www.WASPMuseum.org
Order of Daedalians www.Daedalians.org
Organization of Black Aerospace Professionals www.obap.org
Professional Aviation Maintenance Association www.PAMA.org
Professional Women Controllers, Inc. www.pwcinc.org
Remote Pilot Council-Association for Unmanned Vehicle Systems
    International https://www.auvsi.org/remote-pilots-council
Seaplane Pilots Association www.seaplanepilotsassociation.org
Sisters of the Skies (SOS) www.SistersoftheSkies.org
Society of Women Engineers www.SWE.org
Technical Women's Organization www.TechnicalWomen.org
The Airship Association www.airship-association.org
The Ninety-Nines International Organization of Women Pilots
    www.ninety-nines.org
The Ninety-Nines Museum of Women Pilots
    www.museumofwomenpilots.org
United States Parachute Association www.uspa.org
University Aviation Association www.uaa.aero
Whirly-Girls-International Women Helicopter Pilots
    www.whirlygirls.org
Wings Across America honors Women Airforce Service Pilots
    (WASP) of World War II www.wingsacrossamerica.us
Women in Aerospace (WIA) www.womeninaerospace.org
Women in Aviation International (WAI) www.wai.org
Women in Corporate Aviation (WCA) www.wca-intl.org

Women Military Aviators www.womenmilitaryaviators.com
Women Soaring Pilots Association www.womensoaring.org
Women Who Drone www.womenwhodrone.co
Women's Skydiving Network www.womeninskydiving.org

(Flight Simulator.. Ann Stricklin photographer.)

Education is what allows you to stand out.
~ Ellen Ochoa, NASA Astronaut.

INDEX

ABOUT THE AUTHOR

In 1982, Dr. Penny Rafferty Hamilton began her newspaper and photography career. She continues to publish in many and varied publications on aviation, health, and women's history. She has won several National and State business and writing awards, including recognition from the U.S. Small Business Administration, National Association of State Aviation Officials, and Colorado Authors' League. She is a Laureate of both the Colorado Aviation and the Women's Halls of Fame. She is a graduate of Temple University, Columbia College (Distinguished Alumna Award Winner), and the University of Nebraska (Alumni Achievement Award Winner).

She is a member of numerous aviation and writers organizations. A General Aviation pilot, she co-holds a World's Aviation Speed Record with her husband, William. With advanced degrees and extensive broadcast experience, she is a frequent speaker for the aviation industry with a passion for women's and aviation history.

Other books by Penny Rafferty Hamilton, Ph.D.

America's Amazing Airports (2019)

A to Z: Your Grand County History Alphabet (2017)

Absent Aviators: Gender Issues in Aviation (Chapter contributor) 2014, paperback 2020.

Arcadia Images of America: *Around Granby* (2013)

Granby, Then & Now: 1905-2005 (2005)

Contributor to: *Capture My Colorado and also, Country Woman's Christmas 2011.*

Her web sites are:

www.PennyHamilton.com and www.TeachingWomentoFly.com

(Dr. Penny Rafferty Hamilton dressed as historic aviator, Harriet Quimby in purple satin flying suit. Photo by Colorado Women's Hall of Fame/Kit Williams)